The celebrated film director François Truffaut once famously observed that there was a certain incompatibility between the terms British and cinema. That was typical of the critical disparagement for so long suffered by British films. As late as 1969 a respected film scholar could dub British cinema 'the unknown cinema'. This was the situation because up to that time the critics, scholars and intellectuals writing about cinema preferred either continental films or latterly Hollywood to the homegrown product. Over the past thirty years that position has changed dramatically. There are now monographs, journals, book series, university courses and conferences entirely devoted to British cinema.

The Tauris British Film Guide series seeks to add to that process of revaluation by assessing in depth key British films from the past hundred years. Each film guide will establish the historical and cinematic context of the film, provide a detailed critical reading and assess the reception and after-life of the production. The series will draw on all genres and all eras and will over time build into a wide-ranging library of informed, in-depth books on the films that have defined British cinema. It is a publishing project that will comprehensively refute Truffaut's ill-informed judgement and demonstrate the variety, creativity, humanity, poetry and mythic power of the best of British cinema.

JEFFREY RICHARDS
General Editor, the British Film Guides

British Film Guides published and forthcoming:

The Charge of the Light Brigade Mark Connelly
The Dam Busters John Ramsden
Dracula Peter Hutchings
My Beautiful Laundrette Christine Geraghty
A Night to Remember Jeffrey Richards
The Private Life of Henry VIII Greg Walker
The Red Shoes Mark Connelly
The 39 Steps Mark Glancy
Whisky Galore! and The Maggie Colin McArthur

A BRITISH FILM GUIDE

The Dam Busters

JOHN RAMSDEN

I.B. TAURIS

LONDON · NEW YORK

Published in 2003 by I.B.Tauris & Co Ltd
6 Salem Road, London w2 4BU
175 Fifth Avenue, New York NY 10010
www.ibtauris.com

In the United States of America and Canada distributed by Palgrave
Macmillan a division of St Martin's Press, 175 Fifth Avenue, New York
NY 10010

ISBN 1 86064 636 0

A full CIP record for this book is available from the British Library
A full CIP record for this book is available from the Library of Congress

Library of Congress catalog card: available

Set in Monotype Fournier and Univers Black by Ewan Smith, London
Printed and bound in Great Britain by MPG Books, Bodmin

Contents

Illustrations

Acknowledgements

Working on this book has been a treat for one who in the past has worked mainly on the drier zones of political history, but who here was able to revisit and re-examine youthful enthusiasms. It reignited memories of a childhood spent in an insalubrious Sheffield cinema (long since closed), and of an eight-year-old self trying to play 'The Dam Busters' March' on the piano (loud but not accurate). I cannot thank Jeffrey Richards enough for giving me the opportunity, and for his helpful advice on the book when in draft.

The sources on which the book relies are listed in notes and at the end, but it would be remiss of me not to offer a special thanks to Michael Anderson, George Baker, Bill Kerr and Richard Todd, for sharing with me their memories of the making of the film, to the library of the British Film Institute for advice on sources, and to the National Library of Australia and the BECTU History Project for permission to quote from material in which they hold the copyright. It was most helpful to see an advance draft of Mark Connelly's chapter on Bomber Command in British films, and I also owe thanks for advice on content to James Chapman, Mark Glancy and Vincent Porter. I derived much help when drafting the article which sparked my interest in the topic from Bob Cole at Utah State University, David Blackbourn at Harvard, and several members of Paul Kennedy's research seminar at Yale, none of whom can have been aware how helpful they were actually being or how long it would take to bear fruit, such is academic life. To all of these I am most grateful.

All photographs are by courtesy of the Library of the British Film Institute except no. 9, which comes from the *News Chronicle*. The stills are reproduced here for the purposes of critical analysis.

Film Credits

THE DAM BUSTERS

Director	Michael Anderson
Production Company	Association British Pictures Corporation
Studio	Elstree; location work at RAF Scampton, RAF Hemswell and Trafalgar Point (all Lincolnshire), and various dams and reservoirs including Derwent Valley (Derbyshire) and Elan Valley (Powys)
Director in charge of production	Robert Clark
Production Supervisor	W. A. Whittaker
Production Manager	Gordon C. Scott
Assistant Director	John Street
Continuity	Thelma Orr
Casting Directors	Robert Lennard and G. B. Walker
Screenplay	R. C. Sherriff, based on the book by Paul Brickhill and on Wing Commander Gibson's own account in *Enemy Coast Ahead*
Director of Photography	Erwin Hillier
Special Effects Photography	Gilbert Taylor
Camera Operator	Norman Warwick
Special Effects	George Blackwell
Editor	Richard Best
Art Director	Robert Jones
Make-up	Stuart Freeborn
Hairdresser	Hilda Winifred Fox
Music	Leighton Lucas; 'The Dambusters' March' by Eric Coates
Music performed by	Associated British Studio Orchestra, conducted by Louis Levy
Recording Director (Music)	H. V. King
Sound Recording	Leslie Hammond
Dubbing Editor	Arthur Southgate
Technical Adviser	J. N. H. Whitworth
Unit Car Driver	Eddie Frewen
Format	35mm
Length	11,230 feet

Running Time	124 minutes (continental and US versions: 101 minutes)
Première	16 May 1955
General release date	5 September 1955

CAST (AS LISTED IN FINAL CREDITS)

Michael Redgrave	Dr Barnes N. Wallis, CBE, FRS
Ursula Jeans	Mrs Wallis
Charles Carson	Doctor
Stanley Van Beers	Dr David Pye (now Sir David Pye, CB, FRS)
Colin Tapley	Dr W. H. Glanville, CB, CBE
Frederick Leister, *Eric Messiter* and *Laidman Brown*	Committee Members
Raymond Huntley	Official, National Physical Laboratory
Hugh Manning	Official, Ministry of Aircraft Production
Patrick Barr	Captain Joseph 'Mutt' Summers, CBE
Edwin Styles and *Hugh Moxey*	Observers at Trials
Anthony Shaw	RAF Officer at Trials
Basil Sydney	Air Chief Marshal Sir Arthur Harris, GCB, OBE, AFC (now Marshal of the RAF)
Ernest Clark	Air Vice Marshal the Hon. Ralph Cochrane, GBE, KCB, AFC (now Air Chief Marshal)
Derek Farr	Group Captain J. N. H. Whitworth, DSO, DFC
Laurence Naismith	Farmer
Harold Siddons	Group Signals Officer
Frank Phillips	BBC Announcer

Members of 617 squadron

Richard Todd	Wing Commander Guy Gibson, VC, DSO, DFC
Brewster Mason	Flight Lieutenant R. D. Trevor-Roper, DFC, DFM
Anthony Doonan	Flight Lieutenant R. E. G. Hutchison, DFC
Nigel Stock	Flying Officer F. M. Spafford, DFC, DFM
Brian Nissen	Flight Lieutenant R. D. Taerum, DFC
Robert Shaw	Flight Sergeant J. Pulford, DFM
Peter Assinder	Pilot Officer G. R. Deering, DFC
Richard Leech	Squadron Leader H. M. Young, DFC
Richard Thorp	Squadron Leader H. E. Maudslay, DFC
John Fraser	Flight Lieutenant J. V. Hopgood, DFC
David Morell	Flight Lieutenant W. Astell, DFC
Bill Kerr	Flight Lieutenant H. B. Martin, DSO, DFC, AFC (now Wing Commander)

George Baker	Flight Lieutenant D. J. H. Maltby, DSO, DFC
Ronald Wilson	Flight Lieutenant D. J. Shannon, DSO, DFC
Denys Graham	Flight Lieutenant L. G. Knight, DSO
Basil Appleby	Flight Lieutenant R. G. Hay, DFC
Tim Turner	Flight Lieutenant J. F. Leggo, DFC
Ewen Solon	Flight Sergeant G. E. Powell
Harold Goodwin	Wing Commander Gibson's batman

UNCREDITED ACTORS

Peter Arne	RAF Officer, 57 squadron
Richard Coleman	RAF Officer, 57 squadron
Gerald Harper	RAF Officer, 57 squadron
Arthur Howard	Pay Officer, RAF Scampton
Lloyd Lamble	A. R. Collins, Road Research Laboratory
Edwin Richfield	RAF Personnel Officer, 5 Gr

Introduction

Early in the morning of 17 May 1943, a squadron of Lancaster bombers, belonging to 617 squadron and operating out of RAF Scampton in Lincolnshire, carried out 'Operation Chastise', successfully attacking the Mohne and Eder dams in Germany's Ruhr region. Both dams were breached to the extent that major flooding took place, and the Allied press around the world was convinced that a heavy blow had been struck at Germany's war economy, a blow that would contribute signally to shortening the war. Stalin telegraphed his congratulations and Churchill was cheered to the echo when he mentioned the raid in an address to the US congress two days later.[1]

617 squadron was promptly christened 'the dam busters' (motto: 'Après moi, le déluge'), though they were used for the remainder of the war mainly on other bombing tasks requiring exceptional precision. The squadron had succeeded in its original raid only at great cost: eight of its nineteen bombers did not return, fifty-four crew-members were killed, and, although the squadron's legendary commanding officer Wing Commander Guy Gibson was one of the survivors, he too was killed during a raid in the following year. The dams raid made a great media impact, and after 1945 news gradually seeped out that it had not only been a triumph for the skills and heroism of Bomber Command's young men, but also, through their use of a new and technologically amazing 'bouncing-bomb', thought up by the scientist and inventor Barnes Wallis, a triumph too for British ingenuity and scientific know-how.

More than fifty years later, in a competition in which thousands of viewers cast votes, a television advertisement for Carling Black Label lager, first shown in 1989, was ranked among the most effective television advertisements of all time – only just behind Nicole with her Renault, Nick Kamen's Levi's and Leonard Rossiter tipping Martinis over Joan Collins. The advert shows a German soldier patrolling a dam wall on a (black-and-white) moonlit night, suddenly made aware by the drone of engines of the approach of bombers. The sentry quickly strips off his coat, and performs miracles of goalkeeping as bombs bounce towards him across the water. The twin towers of the dam have become goalposts, but as the soundtrack booms out a familiar tune the keeper maintains his clean sheet. In 1943, it was the British bouncing-bombs that reached parts that other bombs could not reach; in 1989 a Danish beer saved the day for the home team.

In recent years sales seem to continue for a children's book which ingeniously reworked the 1943 story with dive-bombing super-chickens seeing off predatory foxes with both low flying and a miracle bomb – though in a dramatic change from 1943, all the best dive-bombers in *The Fox Busters* are girls. These chickens can also read, and so name their chicks after words visible in the farmyard, mainly tractor and feed suppliers, but it cannot be entirely coincidental that their father figure is called Massey-*Harris* or that his most aerobatic offspring is called Ransome ('Arthur' perhaps?). Arthur 'Bomber' Harris, through the agency of the *Fox Busters*, therefore lives on for another generation of the young – or at least entertains their fathers while they are being read to sleep.[2]

A different type of homage is paid by George Lucas's first *Star Wars* film (1977), which not only has several quotations from the raid sequences of *The Dam Busters* script during its own climactic air raid, but also makes visual quotations in the framing of some aerial attack sequences (for example, two attacking planes fly over the camera, and an anti-aircraft gun swivels across the frame to follow their flight path). *The Dam Busters* was indeed studied by the *Star Wars* production team as a basis for setting up its low-flying sequences, an influence that no doubt owed a good deal to its cinematographer Gilbert Taylor who had himself worked on the second unit of the 1955 film as special effects photographer. Such are the hidden continuities of cinema history, visible only to those who scan to the very depths of the credits list.

Few of those who voted in that television poll in the year 2000, or read *The Fox Busters* to their children, or saw *Star Wars* when it came out, can have been old enough to have any personal memory of the 1943 raid, but the point of the advertisement – and of another lager advert in which British skills once again 'defeated' the Germans – could only have been grasped because the mass television audience already knew about those events of 1943, and would therefore recognize what was being parodied. Expensive television advertisements are not filmed and networked without prior audience research to prove their effectiveness, which in this case would need to have included familiarity with the 1943 dams raid. A majority of those television viewers in 2000 cannot have been old enough to visit the cinema in 1955, even to see a film classified for showing to audiences of all ages. Yet it is *The Dam Busters*, the outstanding British film of 1955 – and especially through its annual reshowings on television for the past quarter-century – that explains the continuity between what actually happened in 1943 and what the public know about it over fifty years later.

The Dam Busters was that modern British rarity, a film released to critical acclaim that was also popular with the public. During the 1950s, when war films were all the rage, *The Dam Busters* was the pinnacle of the genre, a film of higher quality and deeper meaning which deserved its prizes as well as its earnings. It was a film which defied the conventions of screen success – it had no significant role for a woman, a mere thirty seconds of glamour in a two-hour film, and few established names in the cast – but it became the major box-office earner of the year in Britain. Yet while very successful in the Commonwealth as well as in the United Kingdom, *The Dam Busters* flopped in the all-important American market and has faded completely from the memory there. At a 1995 Harvard seminar of historians who specialize in modern British history, there were only two present who had ever seen the film – and they were both from Yorkshire.

This book will try to explain what lay behind such a record, seeking to explain the film's great but differential impact when released in 1955, and why it lived on in the British memory thereafter. And since it has been influential in shaping popular perceptions of the real raid of 1943, of Britain's bombing offensive against Germany, and to an extent of the whole war, it will also be asked how accurate it was meant to be – and how accurate it actually was – as a historical record. For this, we must begin in 1943, with the raid itself.

ONE
The Historical Background

THE RAID AND ITS SIGNIFICANCE

As the film is considered scene by scene in Chapter 3, its accuracy as compared to what is now known about the events of 1943 will be assessed; this chapter considers only the bigger issues. The bomb explosions in the early hours of 17 May 1943 were so powerful as to register with devices installed to measure earthquakes, and the breaching of the Mohne and Eder dams caused a commensurate amount of damage to life and property. Since the Mohne dam was almost full and the valley below was steep and narrow, the effects there were the greater. The chief engineer at the power station, who had himself given warnings of the danger, now witnessed a catastrophe, including the drowning of half a dozen relatives, which he was powerless to prevent. The dam was breached across a length of over 200 feet and to a depth of 22 feet, and within twelve hours over 100 million cubic metres of water flowed out and rushed down the valley, destroying bridges, factories and homes, drowning 1,294 people (nearly two-thirds of them slave workers from Holland and the Ukraine) and over 6,000 cattle and pigs. A breach of a similar size in the Eder dam caused even more water to flood the valleys as far away as Bremen, 400 kilometres downstream; a cameraman grimly recorded milk being delivered by boat to houses 139 kilometres from the ruined reservoir. As the valley was wider and less steep, the Eder's water did less immediate damage, causing only forty-seven deaths, but the area of ruined farmland, of damaged bridges and factories, and of transport chaos, was wider. At the other end of the world, a Melbourne paper crowed that 'Kassel looks like Venice from the air'.[1] In a fine example of 'propaganda with facts', the RAF dropped thousands of enlarged copies of reconnaissance photographs of the breached Mohne dam in Germany and across occupied Europe.

Total casualties were roughly similar to the highest number of civilian deaths caused in London on the worst night of the 1940–41 bombing, while the death total on the night that Coventry was 'destroyed' in 1941 was 568. So although the number of human casualties in the dams raid was low compared to those suffered later in the war by other German cities, it was far from inconsiderable when compared to Britain's own level of civilian suffering.

The immediate economic impact of the raid was also considerable. Munitions production in the Ruhr valley was brought almost to a standstill, transport in the area brought to a halt, and the Nazi leaders' own initial view was that their war economy had suffered a 'catastrophe'. Schoolchildren and army units were drafted in to help clear up the mess, and within forty-eight hours up to ten thousand additional workers (many again slave labourers) were on their way to the area to begin the more lasting work of reconstruction. But Albert Speer, organizer of Hitler's war economy, soon reported that water supplies could be back to normal within a few weeks, while munitions production would return to half of normal levels within five days of the raid and to normal levels a week later. Joseph Goebbels happily recorded in his diary that 'Speer is truly a management genius'.[2] Initial press reports in neutral countries such as Sweden, Switzerland and Morocco, that the raid had seriously weakened German morale, had increased to danger levels public grumbling against the government, and might even bring down the Nazi regime, soon therefore proved illusory. As the year 1943 wore on, the dams themselves were repaired, repair work that could not be interrupted by further bombing once defensive obstacles and artillery were in place. A later attempt in autumn 1944 to breach the Sorpe dam (the biggest target of the 1943 raid not hit successfully) with another Wallis invention, the 12,000-pound 'tallboy' bomb, proved abortive, and that dam too survived to assist the German war economy until it was overrun by the Allied armies. Wallis then in 1945 immediately visited the Mohne and found that only one bouncing-bomb had actually hit the target properly (causing the breach) and that repairs since 1943 seemed to have been effective. There is no doubt then that Allied hopes that the raid would be so important as to cripple Germany and shorten the war were well wide of the mark. An official history of the RAF was already concluding in 1953 that 'the damage caused, though great was not decisive; industry in the Ruhr received a heavy, but by no means a mortal, blow'.[3]

Occupying British forces in 1945 must also soon have discovered that one of the 'bouncing-bombs' had been 'captured alive' by the German authorities in 1943, even though the Lancaster carrying it had crashed in flames, and that German scientists had worked out within a month most of the principles that made it work. Ironically, the Germans' own problems with sceptical scientific bureaucrats ensured that a similar German weapon was never used in retaliation against British reservoirs. Nevertheless, although the recent enemy already had them, a cautious British government kept many of the weapon's details as classified information for the next twenty years, insisting on referring to the weapon as a 'mine', or as a 'bouncing-bomb' (which it was not) even though the Germans had correctly divined in 1943 that it was actually a spinning depth charge: back-spin made it skip over the water and slide down the face of the dam, while a hydrostatic fuse made it explode at the right depth. The 1955 film was naturally constrained by these decisions relating to national security – for example, it shows the bombs as the wrong shape, more spherical than cylindrical. It makes no mention at all of the fact that they were back-spun before being dropped.

Since 1943, the value of the raid has been much questioned. Its critics have concentrated on three lines of attack. First, the number of casualties inflicted on civilians; second, the RAF's alleged incompetence in aiming at the wrong target (in particular failing to give a high enough priority to the Sorpe dam); and third, the apparent brevity of any effect on the German economy, compared to the loss of so many experienced British aircrew. The first point is easily dealt with, for in a war where every combatant quite deliberately and routinely caused civilian casualties by bombing, this raid was without doubt *aimed* at strategic targets. The charge relating to RAF planners missing the Sorpe (a claim based heavily on one document in the files of the Ministry of Economic Warfare, on which too much reliance has been placed) is also effectively rebutted by John Sweetman. RAF files show clearly enough that the importance of hitting the Sorpe as well as the Mohne (so inundating the Ruhr valley with two tides of water and depriving its works of both sources of supply) was well understood. They did not succeed mainly because only one of the five planes sent to attack it ever got beyond the Dutch coast (a fate that could have happened to any bombing mission), though there was, while the raid was in progress, operational confusion over the rerouting of reserve planes to fill the gap (so that they either got there too late or did not get there at all). But this was an understandable failure to correct a piece of bad luck in action, not poor planning or a failure to understand which targets most mattered.[4] Finally, as Sweetman and others have suggested, the quick recovery of the Ruhr industries was possible only through the diversion to it of massive resources of manpower and reconstruction materials (steel, concrete and so on) that

would otherwise have been used elsewhere.[5] The redeployment into
Germany, in May 1943, of units from the Todt slave-labour organization
is a case in point, for that massive civil engineering machine was otherwise concentrating on building defences in northern France to prevent
an Allied invasion. The biggest beneficiaries of the dams raid may thus
have been the Allied soldiers who waded ashore on D-Day in 1944,
since they landed in Normandy, one of the zones for which defences
were not completed by June 1944, because of interruptions in the previous summer.

Defenders of the raid have not limited themselves to refuting these
three attacks, but have added to their rebuttals a claim that, even if the
critics had made good their three claims, the raid would still have been
worthwhile for its impact on morale. Nineteen forty-three was a bad
year for Britain and for Britain's standing with its Allies, an interminable
wait between the 'end of the beginning' in late 1942 and the 'beginning
of the end' in spring 1944. Britain, it is argued, needed a lift, a spectacular
coup that showed what the country could do to the enemy in its very
heartland, and that lift was worth the cost in casualties (this is explicitly
the way in which one of the final survivors of the original 617 squadron
summed up the balance sheet for a recent television documentary).[6]
Moreover, the Russians were impressed by the skill and daring showed
by the dam busters, and so were the Americans – this much is in-
disputable. The raid therefore gave Britain's leaders valuable leverage
in summit-level planning. This is a seductive argument of much merit,
but to argue that the raid was 'worth it' in terms of the casualties suffered
by the RAF (not to mention Germans and their slave-labourers), is in
the end unprovable, for there is no tariff by which we can measure
human lives against something as intangible as morale. Here the film
was anyway important in its own right, for as the public memory of the
raid has increasingly become a memory of the film, Guy Gibson's
cinematic assurance that the young men of 617 squadron would willingly
have died for what they achieved weighs heavily on the mind. It has
now become impossible to detach film from reality and reach a balanced
view on the one without being influenced by the other.

In 1955, of course, things were much less complicated, for as the
film's reviews showed there were few in Britain who then doubted that
the raid had helped to win the war for Britain, very few who complained
about the number of German casualties, and practically nobody who
thought it had not been 'worth it'. As Martin Jackson wrote recently:

In the 50s, there was justifiable pride in the events portrayed in the film, a certainty in the purpose of the war, which it is difficult to understand today, and a genuine sense of community. In 1953 it did not matter a damn whether *The Dam Busters'* raid was success or folly, or whether Allied bombing tactics in general were justified.[7]

The problem is that by making such a fine film, so closely tied to the historical story of acts of recent heroism, under the influence of the mood that Jackson describes, the film-makers may have made it impossible properly to evaluate the raid, or 'Allied bombing tactics in general', even when fifty years of hindsight became available. There may have been few doubts about the justness of the dams raids in the 1950s, but there were already considerable doubts about Allied bombing tactics in general, as we shall see, and these the film helped to stifle.

THE RAID IN MEMORY, 1943–55

There were high hopes when the dams raid was launched. Air Marshal Sir Arthur Harris recalled in 1947 that 'everyone who knew about the operation beforehand, including Winston Churchill, expected much from it and was in a considerable state of excitement on the night that it occurred'. When confirmation of success came through, Harris immediately contacted the White House to let Churchill know the good news, noting (again in 1947) that 'such a disaster, brought about by only nineteen aircraft, must undoubtedly have caused great alarm and despondency in Germany'.[8]

News of the successful raid on the dams was first broadcast by the BBC on the morning of 17 May, soon after the surviving Lancasters returned to Scampton, and during the rest of the day more and more information was released by the Air Ministry, including information about Gibson and quotations from survivors' accounts of the raid, together with reconnaissance photographs, showing breaches in the dams and the flooded valley. Letters and telegrams of congratulation flowed in from politicians, senior RAF officers and civilian scientists. National and provincial newspapers on 18 May made it the major story, convinced that they were reporting a turning point in the war. The *Daily Mail*, for example, breathlessly informed its readers that 'two mighty walls of water were last night rolling irresistibly down the Ruhr and Eder valleys. Railway bridges, power stations, factories, whole villages and built-up areas were being swept away ... No man-made defence can stand in their way.' After listing the cities and towns still at risk – Dortmund, Bochum, Essen, Kassel – the paper's air correspondent added that 'it is quite impossible to predict where the damage will end … The devastation done to Germany's war machine has probably only just begun.' The *Illustrated London News* reported a 'titanic blow at Germany'. MPs in the Commons cheered Air Secretary Sinclair's report, and a week later a backbencher asked facetiously if it was true 'that Herr Hitler is building an ark against the flood in the Ruhr'.

Britain's allies were equally enthusiastic. The Combined Chiefs of Staff were officially informed of the success of the raid on 17 May and on the following day Admiral Leahy on behalf of the Americans was congratulating the British 'on the success of the RAF force in this operation'. The *New York Times*, basing its report on sources in Switzerland, wrote enthusiastically that 'the RAF has secured another triumph. With unexampled daring, skill and ingenuity it has blasted two of Germany's important water dams which are vital parts of the whole industrial and transportation system of West Germany, and has thereby delivered the most devastating single blow dealt from the air.'[9] CBS radio described the dams raid as 'one of the most daring and devastating raids of the war', and reported that Germany was diverting massive resources of manpower to relief and rebuilding work. Churchill was by chance due to address the US Congress on 19 May and he did not miss the opportunity both to enhance British prestige and to restate the case for strategic bombing:

> The condition to which the great centres of German war industry, and particularly the Ruhr, are being reduced is one of unparalleled devastation. You have just read of the destruction of the great dams which feed the canals and provide the power to the enemy's munitions works. That was a gallant operation, costing eight out of the nineteen Lancaster bombers employed, but it will play a very far-reaching part in reducing the German munition output … Wherever their centres [of war industry] exist or are developed, they will be destroyed.[10]

British propagandists in the USA redoubled their efforts to use the raid's success as a way of building up American respect for Britain's contribution to the war effort: in August, Guy Gibson was sent to tour North America for the propaganda campaign, and while in Washington he received the American Legion of Merit (the only other British wartime recipients being Generals Alexander and Montgomery; Gibson was in the summer of 1943 the most decorated member of the entire British armed forces). This propaganda posting was also the only way the RAF could get him to stop flying, but it was not one for which he was ideally suited. Churchill had personally to warn him to guard his tongue after he was heard explaining that breaching the dams must have caused 'a great many casualties – and a good job too!' (He had also candidly explained in the same talk on the *Queen Mary* that when big cities were raided the bombers hardly tried to hit military targets: 'We just plonk them down in the middle of the town.') Once the tour proper began, though, Gibson proved an adept handler of the press, and was especially welcomed in Canada, never failing to stress the Canadian contribution to the raid. He remained a well-known figure for the short remainder of his life, receiving the Victoria Cross, writing his autobiography, and appearing on the BBC's *Desert Island Discs* as one of its earliest 'castaways'. Searching around for something appropriate to do when the war ended, he became the Conservatives' prospective parliamentary candidate for Macclesfield in March 1944, attended the first (and much-reported) annual reunion of 617 squadron in May. But Gibson was restless to fly again, wangled his way back into operations and was shot down over Holland in September.

Official recognition was not limited to Gibson. The King and Queen personally visited Scampton on 27 May, inspected the squadron, and shared jokes with them too, an event captured on *Gaumont British News* for the cinema-going public. It was George VI who chose the squadron's new badge from among the various designs that Gibson had produced, including a not entirely tasteful motto, 'Après moi le déluge', accepted by the College of Arms only when told that the King had already given his approval. In addition to Gibson's VC, the squadron was awarded five DSOs, ten DFCs and four bars, two Conspicuous Gallantry Medals and twelve DFMs. At the investiture at Buckingham Palace on 22 June, these awards were all taken together at the start of the ceremony, so that the honouring of 617 squadron emphasized a team effort. On the same evening, Vickers gave a commemorative dinner in London, and Gibson was photographed signing his name across an enlarged photograph of the breached Mohne dam, the only slip in elaborately formal proceedings being the menu cards' heading: 'The Damn Busters'.

As the war ended, it is unlikely that that raid of 1943 would have faded from memory, but the public had a timely reminder from the posthumous publication in February 1946 of Gibson's autobiography, *Enemy Coast Ahead*, following serialization in the *Sunday Express*. There is some mystery about the book's provenance, and some have doubted whether Gibson wrote it, but even before he formed 617 squadron, he had been assigned by RAF 5 Group the task of writing a book for the instruction of younger pilots – not a technical manual but a prose work about motivation and attitude. He recalls in *Enemy Coast Ahead* that he approached this task with trepidation, since he had done nothing like it before, as well as resenting being placed in such a backwater – from which the dams raid rescued him for a time. Susan Ottaway briskly dismisses in her biography *Dambuster* any doubt about the book's author-ship: 'It has been suggested by some that Guy did not actually write this book, but that it was "ghosted" for him by some anonymous person. Those who knew him well categorically refute this suggestion and it seems almost certain that the book is his own work.' She adds that 'it carries the hallmarks of his sense of humour and is a fine book'. Internal evidence – details only he could have known, attitudes confirmed by friends, a breezy manner with prose that is very like his recorded speeches – certainly fits with Gibson being the author. Richard Morris's biography shows, however, that the original draft, still in the Air Ministry files, was far rougher even than the book eventually published, being 'full of intolerant asides, insubordinate comments, gnomic criticisms, social prejudices, wicked jokes, and – in places – sheer bad writing'. The censors, and probably a literary assistant, helped to turn this manuscript into the book we know.[11]

Gibson started to write an autobiography in early 1944, but did not finish it before his death; the book does not cover anything that happened in the last eighteen months of his life, though the rest of the war is covered in considerable detail. His death obviously deprived him of the chance to polish the manuscript, which would have passed to Eve Gib-son, his widow, though she had become so distant from her husband in 1943–44 that they were planning a divorce when he was killed, and she could hardly have got the book out without support from Guy's sur-viving friends and professional admirers. The book eventually appeared with a foreword by Sir Arthur Harris and clearly had the official support of the RAF, which would have had to clear it on security grounds. All of this matters because of the artful way in which the book is con-structed, the ideological messages that it carries and its duality as both an autobiography and a pilot's history of Bomber Command. The immediacy of the account is given greater impact by the fact that Gibson cannot yet tell all. His book therefore never says what the magic weapon actually did or how it was released from the bomber, and though it cites names where these were already known (Harris, for example), it is coy over the backroom boys. Barnes Wallis, the secondary hero of Gibson's account of the dams raid, remains in anonymity as 'Dr Jeff' (not even an especially imaginative soubriquet when it is remembered that Wallis's assistant was actually called Jeffree), while the test-pilot Captain Summers is given only his flyers' nickname 'Mutt'.

Literary artfulness appears in *Enemy Coast Ahead* in the way in which the reader's appetite is whetted for the key event, the dam-busting raid of 1943. The first chapter, 'Flight Out', describes the hours before take-off, the bombers' flight across the sea, and their approach to that 'enemy coast ahead', but Gibson's authorial voice tells us that he was just then thinking about his past life, and this becomes (in a device almost like a filmscript itself) the pretext for fourteen chapters of flashback in which he describes his war up to April 1943. The book then continues with three chapters describing the formation of 617 squadron, preparation and training, and the raid on the dams, breaking off as Gibson's own bomber leaves the enemy coast behind on its way home. It actually ends (after jejune comments on the need for a strong foreign policy, defence preparations and respect for 'our great Allies who have made the chance of victory possible' – ideas to which the book has never previously referred) with the bathetic, 'We would be coming back'.[12] The book is therefore hardly an autobiography, for it covers only September 1939 to May 1943, less than four years of Gibson's short span of twenty-six.

There is certainly a strong authorial tone to the book that seems very like the Gibson that others knew, and in a preface to a later edition 617 squadron veteran 'Mick' Martin was careful to describe it as 'Guy Gibson's personal account'. It is not always what the RAF establishment might have liked to read, and the fact that some of the book's rougher passages remain in the published text, even if they are then explained away, is in itself strong testament to the book being Gibson's own account. It is, for example, unforgiving of both Germans and critics of bombing: he writes of the later phase of the war that,

> now it was the Germans' turn to moan. In fact they were now squealing and wailing and appealing to the Pope to stop the bombing. Did they remember Warsaw, Rotterdam, Belgrade, Coventry, Bristol, Glasgow, Swansea and London? Did they remember Hitler's threat to raze every British city to the ground, to destroy Great Britain's population? If they did not they had short memories – but that is typical of the Hun.[13]

The book is also full of accounts of partying and heavy drinking, something for which Gibson was known long before the war, but which became more pronounced under the strain of command. At times this can be fairly presented as young men's high spirits, hence rugby scrums in the mess, letting off fire-extinguishers and the like. The cumulative impact of such scenes, sometimes associated with driving at dangerous speeds and other anti-social activities off the base, does create a negative impact on the reader. Gibson explains that such behaviour was a crucial safety-valve for young men living with the actuality of their friends' deaths and the probability of their own; but Arthur Harris's foreword takes no chances, warning the reader of what lies ahead and placing the blame quite elsewhere:

> It may well be that the references to 'parties' and 'drunks' in this book will give rise to criticism, and even to outbursts of unctuous rectitude. I do not attempt to excuse them, if only because I entirely approve of them. In any case, the 'drunks' were mainly on near-beer and high rather than potent spirits. [This is hard to square with Gibson's accounts of downing more than ten pints of beer at a session, and of mixing cocktails of rum and whisky.]
>
> Remember that these crews, shining youth on the threshold of life, lived under circumstances of intolerable strain. They were in fact – and they knew it – faced with the virtual certainty of death, probably in one of its least pleasant forms. They knew, well enough, that they owed their circumstances to the stupidity, negligence and selfishness of the older generations who had since 1918 done little to avert another war and even less to prepare for it.[14]

Harris concludes, with a neat tribute: 'If there is a Valhalla, Guy Gibson and his band of brothers will be found there at all the parties, seated far above the salt.'

The book is also not quite a conventional autobiography in the way in which it parallels Gibson's own experiences with the learning processes of Bomber Command. He begins in 1939, by which time he had already been a pilot for three years, but had never taken off with a bomb in the bay, and had never landed at night. By the end, his very different squadron is executing a tremendously difficult technical operation, bringing it to success and demonstrating what the RAF as well as Gibson has learned. The book explicitly endorses the development of the Pathfinder squadrons to illuminate targets so that ordinary bombers could hit them without incurring over-heavy casualties, and the role of the 'master bomber' as an over-the-target stage manager (a development that Gibson almost invented by doing just that in the dams raid). The story was thus one of technique, science, training and leadership developing in parallel, but combining to allow a better hit-rate on military targets. No wonder then that the RAF welcomed such a book coming out in 1946 under the name of one of its greatest heroes. It was even helpful that Gibson's book breaks off in May 1943, for it would have been difficult to sustain with evidence from the last two years of the war his core theme, that the technical problems of Bomber Command had been all but solved by mid-1943. Harris naturally drove the point home in his foreword: 'Throughout the story, something is indicated of the difficulties of obtaining the means and the equipment which during the last eighteen months of the war enabled us to find and hit ever smaller objectives, under more and more difficult conditions.'[15]

Gibson's book is, however, very much an autobiography in that it presents a story of RAF operational command. He pays tribute to its senior officers, notably to Harris (though, 'a grim man, is Air Chief Marshal Harris'). He is at pains to pay tribute to the groundstaff and NCOs, who after all made up the overwhelming majority of an RAF squadron – only about 150 of the 700 hundred men and women in the original 617 squadron were flyers, and only two dozen were pilots. These tributes never quite ring true except perhaps when he is describing warrant officers who were themselves carrying heavy responsibilities, and they certainly do not reflect Gibson's habit of bawling out the 'erks' whenever they got in his way; they responded by christening him 'the boy Emperor'. The book is almost wholly about the aircrew with whom Gibson flew, and former flyers now in the higher command. Though he does pay frequent respect to the other members of the Lancasters' crews, it is clearly for pilots that he has the greatest sympathy. In a key passage he reviews the different duties of the pilots of fighters and bombers, coming down heavily against the fighter pilots, who had seemed the more dashing, sexier figures ever since August 1940. Bomber pilots were

> men with responsibility. They have a crew of about seven chaps, all of whom depend on the captain for their lives. They fly aircraft weighing about thirty tons and costing £35,000 sterling ... They face all the hazards of bad weather, icing and low cloud. They have to endure the sagging effect on morale of high casualties due to enemy action; they have to wait weeks, perhaps, to know what happened to their comrades; and all the time weighing on top of them is a deep sense of responsibility ... They soon find that the other members of a squadron, feeling as they do that they captain the 'little ships' of the air, like to take a pride in their

appearance, they like to keep their offices clean and tidy, their gardens growing, their aircraft polished. Such spirit breeds efficiency.

If this is true of the captain of each bomber, it is even truer of the squadron commander, for most of the book Gibson himself. He must socialize with the boys as well as maintain iron discipline, for it is his responsibility both to lead and to maintain morale.

> The one and only plan is to go out with the boys, drink with them, lead them into thinking they are the best, that they cannot die. Get them away from the atmosphere of 'Yes, Sir', 'No, Sir'. But make sure that that atmosphere is very much present next day; be polite, listen to advice … Then you will have high morale and a keen team spirit. Huns will be shot down; bombs will fall on target.[16]

Gibson certainly practised what he preached; when he took over 106 squadron his new men were delighted to find him a good drinking companion in the mess on his first evening, rather less enchanted by the roasting he gave them for not standing to attention when he entered the briefing room the next morning. What deserves notice, however, is the extent to which his book describes a highly elitist view of the bomber offensive. Scientists and officers exercise initiative, groundstaff do what they are told; the key people are the 'captains' of each bomber and the squadron commander, men who both take responsibility *and* risk their own lives. This was, in 1946, already a long way from the democratic manner in which 'the People's War' of 1939–45 had generally been described while it was taking place, but his account was widely read. Gibson's book was regularly reprinted, a paperback coming out to coincide with the 1955 film, and was also officially anthologized in the 1943 *RAF Year Book*, also not published until after the war and incorporating his account of the dams raid.

Gibson's book was well received by reviewers, as was his thesis about Bomber Command: the *Daily Telegraph* referred to Churchill's 'war-winning' intervention to create the Pathfinder unit: 'Then came accuracy, and with it the demolition of pin-point targets, culminating in the attack on the great Mohne Dam which Gibson led.' Likewise, the *Times Literary Supplement* saw Gibson's book as 'The Ghost of Bomber Command', and his life and death as its vindication; it was 'the very idiom and accent of Bomber Command'. The authenticity of Gibson's account then received a formal accolade in Bomber Harris's own memoirs in 1947: 'I cannot add much to the published account of the actual operation against the dams, operation "Chastise", that was written by Wing Commander Guy Gibson before he was killed in action.'[17]

Any danger that the 1943 raid might fade from memory vanished when a true bestseller on the subject was published by Paul Brickhill in 1951. When Brickhill died in 1991, *The Times* concluded that his 'story of Barnes Wallis's unique bouncing bombs breaching the Ruhr dams, thanks to the skill and daring of Wing Commander Guy Gibson and his pilots of 617 squadron, endowed a single air raid with a mythological status it has never lost'. Brickhill was an Australian journalist who joined the Royal Australian Air Force in 1940 and served as a fighter pilot in Britain and the Middle East. He was as much of a daredevil as any of the wartime heroes about whom he subsequently wrote, being for example court-martialled for 'low and dangerous flying' over Bournemouth, after allegedly 'beating up' a pub in his Spitfire (Guy Gibson, in similar spirit, once tried to fly a Hampden bomber *under* the Trent bridge in Nottingham). He was wounded while being shot down in 1943 in Tunisia and spent the rest of the war in the infamous Stalag Luft III, where he was an escape organizer. Even that bald summary of his past career makes clear that he had good insights into the RAF world about which he mainly wrote, but also that he was unlikely to view its leading figures with scepticism or detachment.[18]

While working as a foreign correspondent after 1945, he co-authored *Escape to Danger*, which anthologized the experiences of pilots like himself who had baled out during combat. The book's success persuaded him to become a full-time writer. His first single-authored book, *The Great Escape*, told the story of the mass breakout from Stalag Luft III, which Brickhill had himself helped to organize but in which he had not taken part (fortunately so, since the Germans shot fifty of the seventy-eight escapees). It duly became a classic film in 1963, starring Steve McQueen and Richard Attenborough. This was followed by *The Dam Busters* (book 1951, film 1955) and *Reach for the Sky* (book 1954, film 1956). Together, thought his *Times* obituarist, 'his three best-known books ... may almost be said to constitute an anthology of the cardinal points of wartime heroism as it was received by the generation of schoolboys who grew up in the post-war period'. Thereafter, Brickhill's writing career stalled and he produced little more in the last thirty-five years of his life. His unproductive later years were no doubt consoled by earnings from his books and from the equally successful films based on them. In the case of *The Dam Busters* book, there were regular hardback reprints, inclusion in the first ever *Reader's Digest Condensed*

Edition, a paperback version from Pan in 1954, release in the Companion Book Club (the middle class's mass market hardback outlet in the 1950s), serialization in the *London Evening News* to coincide with the film, and a simplified edition for schoolchildren in 1958. In 1972 there was another edition for teenage boys with reading difficulties (the exciting story presumably intended to engage their minds), and in 1982 an audio version of the book read by Richard Todd. It was revised and updated in 1972, the new edition becoming a paperback in 1983, has remained almost continuously in print since 1951, and in its first half century clocked up sales of over a million copies.

Brickhill's books exhibited certain common features, quite apart from the fact that two were based on – and the third largely around – the young men of the RAF. He wrote lucidly and idiomatically, keeping the pace moving in short sentences and short chapters, incorporating humour whenever possible (often by showing the high-spirited youthfulness of his flyers), and with sharply etched portraits of the officers as the heroes of the war. He also brought the books alive by including passages of direct speech, though this must at times have derived as much from imagination as from the fragile memories of surviving witnesses. The primary virtue for Brickhill was personal courage, whether physical courage in combat or moral courage in wartime adversity, both types stereotypically combined in the legless fighter pilot Douglas Bader's *Reach for the Sky* (played unforgettably by Kenneth More in the film). Brickhill's moral was that success followed refusal to give way to disappointment or defeat; a moral closely related to the national myth of Dunkirk, the Blitz and the Battle of Britain in 1940–41, but restaged as an inherent national trait by Brickhill in the individual war narratives of his books. *The Dam Busters*, he wrote, was 'the story of quality as against quantity, demonstrating that exceptional skill and ingenuity can give one man or one unit the effectiveness of ten. It seems that this is a rather British synthesis of talents, and perhaps this story will reassure those who are dismayed by the fact that the British and their allies are outnumbered in this not too amicable world'.[19] On the other side of the equation, the worst human or national failing for Brickhill was obtuseness, whether of prison guards or of bureaucrats – except that these provided necessary obstacles over which his heroes could prove their mettle. There is, for example, an ironical passage in *The Dam Busters*, ignored by the film, in which the officer responsible for defending the Ruhr dams, 'a certain Oberburgmeister Dillgardt', is shown to have demanded better protection for them, correctly predicting both their vulnerability to aerial attack and the dire consequences of a breach. Dillgardt is ignored by the German authorities much as Wallis is being ignored by the British, and is able in 1943 to say 'I told you so' to chiefs of the Wehrmacht, who now provide additional booms, nets, steel reinforcements and defensive guns to protect the dams when rebuilt. To Brickhill, the difference seems to have been that while Dillgardt eventually gave up making his protests, Wallis and Gibson did not, allowing them to defeat both the forces of obstruction in their own country, and the geographical and military obstacles in Germany. Character thus won in the end – national character.

Brickhill's book is for its first half a single narrative in which he shows how Wallis, beginning as soon as war breaks out in 1939, tries to use his scientific brain to shorten the war and ensure that Britain wins. He sees that a big hit at Germany's energy supplies might cripple its war industries, and be far more effective than many small attacks. He then develops an 'earthquake bomb', though this would be too large for any plane in existence to carry to enemy airspace, and to consider its potential he also has to make himself an expert on dams. From this develops the fixation with dams that leads him to consider getting a bomb to skip over the defences in the reservoir (hence the need to 'bounce' over booms and nets), and sink against the dam wall (so that its explosive power would act like the earthquake bomb in shaking the dam to pieces by the force of its blast). Through all of this he is sometimes encouraged and sometimes obstructed by official scientists in Whitehall, but persists and eventually gets permission for an experimental prototype bomb. This duly bounces as predicted, and film of it is used to convince the authorities to go ahead with a raid on the dams (after Whitehall processes, which Brickhill does not pretend to understand). It will now be a race against time to carry out the raid while the dams are full of winter water – a retrospective swipe at the men of limited vision who have wasted time by not having faith in Wallis earlier.

The focus now shifts to the recruitment and training of a new bombing squadron, initially 'X squadron' since the bureaucracy in the Air Ministry cannot even keep up with finding it a number. Again, a powerful personality, this time Guy Gibson, triumphs over the forces of inertia, and his team is assembled, trained and becomes expert in low flying just in time, while the final technical problems of bomb design, calibrated low-flying in the dark, and accurate bomb-aiming, are each solved by the combined resources and ingenuity of the RAF and its scientific support. The raid itself is described excitingly but unemotionally, attacks being made on all three target dams while tension builds back in Group Control. Heavy losses are sustained by the bomber force, but success crowns their efforts against the Mohne and the Eder. The attack on the Sorpe fails, largely because of the destruction or damage of most of the strike force during the flight out. The main narrative ends with the surviving flyers anxiously awaiting the return to base of comrades who will never in fact show up, but then indulging in a colossal drinking binge that goes on all day (an event that is both tidied up in the film and moved to the evening before the raid rather than the morning after – presumably lest public taste be upset by the apparent callousness of young men partying when their comrades are posted missing). The book describes 617 squadron's surprise at its sudden celebrity status, the shower of decorations, and the royal visit to Scampton and the breezy way in which they respond to such honours; mainly by getting legless, in a sense entirely unrelated to Douglas Bader, on their way to the palace for the investiture.

The second half of the book then covers in considerable detail the later exploits of the squadron, as a 'sniper squadron' for special bombing duties, but with mixed success, and with fewer and fewer of the survivors of 17 May 1943 living to tell the tale. Gibson's crew is killed, and then Gibson himself (though no longer with the squadron) is killed. Ten pilots out of nineteen returned on 17 May 1943, but only half a dozen of these actually survived the war, and this is largely because they were eventually ordered off active operations in July 1944. The second half of the book is therefore quite different from the first – a succession of operations rather than a single event, a pattern which shows the squadron learning ever more sophisticated skills but still largely failing to deliver the knock-out punches that were believed to have struck the Ruhr dams. It becomes increasingly hard for a reader to believe that the mounting casualties in 'the suicide squadron' can be worth such relatively small operational achievements, a downbeat feel that has little in common with reactions to the book's upward-reaching first half. The only human quality left in the end is endurance. Even then, Brickhill notes that although the veterans protested against the decision to end their bombing careers, when it was actually done they became 'changed men, gayer but in a less violent way'. It would be unfair to say that Brickhill's book glorifies war, but he does encourage the reader to respect a particular type of warrior.

In view of this complete contrast between the two halves of Brick-hill's book, it was significant that the film covered only the first, stopping

short of the frantic partying of the day after the great raid, and of the
fame and misfortune that came soon afterwards. For Brickhill, 'the Dam
Busters' meant the squadron of that name; for the film it meant only the
raid. This helpfully allowed a self-contained story to be told in detail
within the space of a single feature film, but it also left out almost all
that was negative, downbeat and depressing in the original book; more
emotional punch is given to the death of a dog and the grieving of its
owner than is ever *shown* for the loss of fifty-six men. In this the film
may not have been far from its sources, for Gibson's father later wrote:
'Guy ... was never happy about the carnage he caused that night – his
main sympathies going out, strangely enough, to the animals, cattle etc
killed.'[20]

Brickhill's book had another significant consequence: it placed for
ever in the spotlight Barnes Wallis and Guy Gibson, even while *saying*
repeatedly that the dams raid had all been a team effort. Gibson's own
book provided a core source for Brickhill and could not be checked with
its author, but it was an unsatisfactory source in several ways, not least
because of the elusiveness of its author as a character in his own right.
While welcoming it, Patrick Gibbs in the *Daily Telegraph* felt that he
still knew little of Gibson the man: 'some Horatio must yet to found "to
report him aright to the unsatisfied", this very antithesis of a Hamlet,
who to our eternal gratitude was all action and no doubt'.[21] Brickhill was
thus Gibson's Horatio, drawing on memories of Gibson from 617
squadron survivors. This was a principle he applied more widely, too,
remarking that 'they were too modest to talk about themselves, so I got
them to tell me about the others, and *vice versa*'.[22] But the problem when
it came to Gibson was that he had in 1943 set out to appear calm, 'all
action and no doubt', as a conscious act of leadership (as he tells us in
his own book), so that collecting his friends' memories without the
chance to cross-check them against his own post-war modesty almost
guaranteed an over-heroic picture. The squadron's adjutant noted in his
log in May 1943 that Gibson seemed 'fit and well and quite unperturbed',
a record of which Gibson himself later remarked, 'this was a complete
lie'. One survivor recalled Gibson as the 'outstanding' influence in the
squadron: 'though we did not see a lot of him he seemed to set a standard
of perfection in all our training and the final preparation. It's called
"leadership" – how do you define it?' There is thus no hint in Brickhill
that Gibson was so run down as to have an unsightly carbuncle on his
face so that he could barely fasten his radio mask – a problem that
Richard Todd certainly does *not* have in the film, despite its passion for

accuracy – or that when he went to the station doctor for treatment he was told that he was not fit to fly, advice that produced a bout of hysterical laughter. When Brickhill's 'Gibson' was transmuted through Todd's finely understated performance, the real Gibson, who was tortured by the strain, the responsibility and the likelihood of death, was probably buried for ever. The later official historian of strategic bombing, Noble Frankland, when he saw *The Dam Busters* as a young man, 'almost imagined that I had seen Guy Gibson. I think I was not alone among British people in feeling that Richard Todd was more like Guy Gibson than Gibson could have been.' This, though, was a sanitized Gibson, and it is impossible to imagine him choosing 'The Ride of the Valkyries' as his favourite piece of music to remind him what a bombing raid was like, as did the real Gibson on *Desert Island Discs*. Richard Morris notes that 'close friends missed the real Gibson's "wicked" humour and unrefined vitality. When asked to name an actor who would have captured the coarser side of Gibson, Ann Shannon [widow of 617 squadron's David Shannon and herself a Scampton WRAF] replied, "Mickey Rooney".'[23]

With Barnes Wallis, the case was more complex. Wallis was a major source for Brickhill, who would have known easily enough how to get the confidence of RAF survivors but was considerably less at home with civil servants and scientists. And since Gibson's book had for security reasons not named Wallis and given only limited information about his work, it was Brickhill's book and the film that made Wallis a household name. Wallis was, however, a difficult man with a permanent sense of grievance about the way in which he had been treated by the scientific establishment and Whitehall. For accuracy, it would have been essential to check Wallis's account with those who had sat on the other side of the desks in the wartime ministries with which he dealt, and this Brickhill seems not to have done. Perhaps he had been influenced by Bomber Harris's memoirs, with their equally negative portrayal of Whitehall bureaucracy. In any event, Brickhill's portrayal of Wallis's lonely crusade against hostile bureaucrats was deeply flawed, but widely believed. This is not to argue that Wallis did not have good reason to feel aggrieved, which he certainly did. There was, for example, the shameful way in which the government denied him the knighthood that Harris recommended two days after the dams raid (Wallis was eventually knighted only in 1967, shortly before he died), fobbing him off instead with a CBE and then only after long delays. It also attempted to avoid paying him anything at all for his wartime inventions, his formal application through the government-appointed award scheme being strongly resisted by the Ministry of Supply. This ought to have put Brickhill on his guard, for men with grievances cannot generally distinguish good grievances from bad ones, and rarely make good witnesses. In due course, this came full circle. Wallis's biographer noted that when Wallis's post-war inventions like the aeroplane *Wild Goose* failed,

> he saw himself once more as the unrecognised, unrewarded and jealously obstructed genius. If the role for which he cast himself was only in part his by right, his claim to it was perversely buttressed by the phenomenal public success of Paul Brickhill's book *The Dam Busters* (and later by the even greater public success of the film made from it). Wherever Wallis went he was greeted as the great scientist who had been forced to fight the authorities in order to be allowed to fight the Germans.

Moreover, 'because of the book he was famous for having no fame. The paradox at one and the same time heightened in him the sense that he was forever the victim of the Fates, and underscored his conviction that the Fates had powerful allies in Whitehall.'[24] This is extremely persuasive, except that it gets the facts the wrong way round: Brickhill's book and the 1955 film were each *products* of Wallis's persecution complex (since he was the source for so much of their story) rather than accidental outside corroborations.

The reality of Wallis's work for the dams raid, placed in its context among the significant contributions of others, can be easily seen in John Sweetman's *The Dambusters Raid*, written when government files had been opened to historians, but Wallis and Brickhill did not go unchallenged even at the time. After seeing the film, Air Marshal Sir Robert Saundby, an ex-Bomber Command staff officer, wrote indignantly to the *New Statesman* (he must have been a very unusual member of the top brass to see that organ as the obvious outlet for officer-class complaints) to point out that the RAF had been planning a raid on the dams for years before Wallis became involved, that many other people in the RAF and civil government had made extremely positive contributions, and (on the basis of his memory) that some of the dialogue was wrong. Brickhill's book, he wrote, was based on a 'fundamental misconception' that Wallis had 'hatched' the idea of a dams raid. Stung by this attack, Brickhill responded at once with two points. First, he dismissed any one man's memory as an unreliable source, claiming that he had only used words reported to him by several witnesses. Second, and less convincingly, he acknowledged that other people had been involved and that RAF planners had thought of the idea of a raid first, but he breezily rejected

('Fiddlesticks!') Saundby's claim that he had therefore got the main story wrong: 'Who cares who first thought there *might* be a way. Both book and film are based on the fundamental fact that Dr. Wallis was the man who "hatched" the only idea that did, in fact, burst dams.'[25] Brickhill had chosen to answer an extreme form of Saundby's charge rather than the actual one: Wallis did indeed 'hatch' the idea that finally worked – after having several others that did not work – but that is not the same as proving that nearly everyone else was blind and unhelpful. Since Brickhill not only wrote the bestselling book, but also then wrote the 'treatment' that Associated British Pictures used as the basis for briefing the screenwriter, it was of course Brickhill's (and Wallis's) view rather than Saundby's that prevailed.

STRATEGIC BOMBING'S UNCOMFORTABLE REPUTATION

The RAF's decision to offer logistical support to *The Dam Busters* film could well have owed something to criticism of Bomber Command since 1943. In the later years of the war, the inability of bombers to hit small strategic targets forced the adoption of tactics of mass destruction instead. There were 1,000-bomber raids on a single city, first directed at Cologne, fire raids of the sort unleashed on Hamburg and Berlin (incendiary bombing specifically designed to cause uncontrollable fires), and the 1945 carpet-bombing of Dresden. The indiscriminate destruction of German cities involved Britain and the United States in a method of war-making that had been condemned when adopted by Germany in 1940, and that in post-war Germany has more often been seen as a war crime than as a legitimate military strategy. Hence German outrage when in the 1990s a statue of Bomber Harris was unveiled in London, outrage all the greater since the statue's unveiler was the Queen Mother, the same Queen Elizabeth who in 1943 had pinned the VC on Guy Gibson's chest.

Even in wartime a few brave voices were raised to condemn Harris's policies – for example, that of Bishop Bell of Chichester in the House of Lords – but the government invariably responded that its objective was to hit military targets rather than to wage war by terror. Nevertheless, as Allied forces and cameramen moved into Germany in 1945, the evidence that accumulated was doubly embarrassing. The scale of destruction became ever more clear, but the results of the US Strategic Bombing Survey (set up precisely to evaluate the effectiveness of strategic bombing as a war weapon) nevertheless found that few bombs had hit their intended target and that the effect of the whole campaign on Germany's war production (at least until the middle of 1944) had been surprisingly small. Already by the war's end, then, there was an uncomfortable feeling that strategic bombing was a campaign of which the Allies should not feel especially proud. When peerages for war services were dished out to all the senior commanders in 1945, the government's decisions not to so reward the chief of Bomber Command, Arthur 'Bomber' Harris, and not to issue a campaign medal for Bomber Command as a whole, were widely seen as a deliberate distancing, the staving off of anticipated criticism. Among Bomber Command veterans this was seen quite differently, as an implied slur on the deaths in action of 55,000 of their comrades.

The growing controversy spurred Harris himself into print with *Bomber Offensive* (1947). In his defence he made exaggerated claims for the results of his work. If, he argued, Bomber Command had had in mid-1943 the equipment that finally arrived in 1944 and had been authorized to launch unlimited attacks, then it was 'an obvious and most certain conclusion' that 'Germany would have been defeated outright by bombing as Japan was'. Such claims produced nervous reviews, not least because they depended on three assumptions which were by then not at all to the taste of the squeamish. First, comparison with Japan's defeat by atom bombs was an uncomfortable reminder that the Allies had been the first to use that dreadfully indiscriminate new weapon. Second, Harris needed a scapegoat for the delays that had prevented a big bomber effort against Germany until 1944–45, and this he found in Whitehall:

> I can recall one civil servant whose whole-hearted devotion to the country and to his work was worth at least a division to the enemy on every day of the war. But for the human limitations of even his devotion to duty and to an eighteen-hour day, he would undoubtedly have been worth two divisions. Luckily he was far from being typical, else we should have perished. Not for nothing was it said in the fighting services that had they only the King's Enemies to deal with – how easy that would be.

Despite the claim that such a figure was a caricature and not typical, everything in Harris's book suggested that he was in fact all too often met with in wartime Whitehall. Since in 1947 it was widely believed that the government machine had done rather well in wartime, this charge too was not welcome.[26]

Finally, he had to prove that in 1944–45 British conventional bombing had indeed devastated German war production. He was on good ground here when he claimed that hundreds of thousands of men permanently deployed to repair bomb damage was in itself a crippling handicap to Germany's war economy (a view very close to the key modern justification of the dams raid). But in trying to refute the findings of the US Strategic Bombing Survey and claim that his own RAF evidence was more reliable, he was driven to quote horrendous figures. US observers found that bombing had destroyed 'only' 31 per cent of houses in Hamburg and 22 per cent in Düsseldorf, but the RAF figures were 61 per cent and 50 per cent respectively. Likewise, 6,427 acres of Berlin had been devastated and 6,200 acres of Hamburg (compared, he notes complacently, to 600 acres of London, 400 in Plymouth and only 100 in Coventry); forty-three of the seventy German cities attacked systematically by Bomber Command had had over half of their surface area devastated.[27] And so on. He needed such evidence for his argument of the effectiveness of the bombing, but once quoted it entirely destroyed his claim that the RAF had in the second half of the war mainly hit small targets accurately.

Paul Brickhill shared Harris's sense that tough wartime decisions were by the late 1940s being judged retrospectively by peacetime standards. He wrote witheringly of a 1944 bombing raid, in which stray bombs demolished houses near a military target,

> Many ordinary people probably died in those crumbled houses, and the post-war domestic moralists, whose virtue increases as the memories of Nazism recede, are likely to point the accusing finger. Most will probably keep pointing it until, Heaven help us, another war starts and their virtue will become tempered by the slightly more powerful instinct of self-survival. A few will continue to point the finger with wistful idealism until one day, perhaps, morals and the practical affairs of man become compatible.[28]

To say the least, by the early 1950s there was no longer a British consensus on the moral correctness of the wartime bombing of Germany.

Brickhill cautiously recognized that the critics of Bomber Command had a case, acknowledging that it was 'still' (in 1951) too rarely admitted that not many British bombs ever hit their intended target. Rather, he says, only about a third of wartime raids ever did real damage: 'Some did none at all, and many people still do not know that.' This admission is, however, turned from negative to positive in the context of 617 squadron, for in May 1943 Gibson and his men were unequivocally aiming at a strategic target, and any deaths were a by-product of success rather than a primary purpose. Moreover, their training to hit a specific target could be represented as the wave of the future, evidence that the RAF had learned from the recent war and would do better if there were to be a next time. This alone would have justified in Brickhill's mind the long grind recounted in the second half of his book to produce and use a really effective, gyroscopic bomb-aiming mechanism, and the development of low-level target identification. 617 squadron's casualties in that effort are in effect presented as deaths in pursuit of a cleaner way of waging future wars. 'The talents that made 617 what they were evolved a new form of precision bombing which enabled a specific military target to be hit accurately and destroyed. Already this is pointing the way towards the end of "carpet" bombing of cities, that dreadfully inescapable feature of recent war.' Use of the word 'inescapable' aligns him clearly with defenders of Bomber Command, but his defence is nevertheless ingenious. It would also have been more effective in the 1950s than it would be now, after four decades during which we have been promised 'smart' bombs but have seen only wars in which bombs still kill civilians. In case his point was missed, it was picked up and amplified in a preface to Brickhill's book by Marshal of the RAF Lord Tedder.

> There have been those who allege that the air weapon is necessarily indiscriminate and that the aim of air power is destruction for the sake of destruction. This book is the story of a team that gave the lie to that allegation; a team whose work had a profound influence on the conduct of air operations, a team whose initiative, skill and self-sacrifice on the one hand saved many an aircrew who would otherwise have been lost on abortive operations, and on the other hand obviated much useless destruction and loss of life in Europe.[29]

Favourable presentation of Harris in *The Dam Busters* was thus the endorsement of a highly controversial figure, and here it departed significantly from the historical record. The real Harris thought the idea of a bouncing bomb to be 'tripe of the wildest description', and 'just about the maddest proposition for a new weapon that we have yet come across'; he was prepared to bet his shirt that 'it will not work, when we have got it'. He had to be ordered to develop and use Wallis's invention, while in the film he becomes a cautious but crucial supporter of the idea. Interestingly, Harris himself had three criticisms of the film's script: that it got details of the raid wrong when they ought to be accurate, that it

exaggerated the importance of Wallis, and that it (wrongly, he claimed)
portrayed Harris himself as an 'irascible, unapproachable moron'.

REVISITING THE WAR ON FILM

Paul Brickhill was one of the most widely read, and about the best, of
the swarm of writers who in the 1950s sought to revisit the recent war;
and it was the popularity of war films – many of them based on the
same bestselling books – with their greater emotive power, that largely
fixed a lasting view of that war for the British people.

The 1950s was still a period in which British cinema could claim an
essentially national audience: overall annual ticket sales fell by a third
between 1948 and 1958, but in 1959 there were still 14.5 million people
a week in British cinemas. This 1959 figure of cinema attendances still
exceeded the number of homes with televisions and almost matched the
total circulation of all national daily newspapers. The crash came in the
1960s as televisions swept into almost every home and cinema's place in
national life was marginalized. Cinema was therefore still a key mass
medium precisely when the war film boom was at its height in the 1950s.
Radio and television celebrated military anniversaries and the publication
of war autobiographies, and presented war heroes telling their own
stories to the microphone and the camera – as both Montgomery and
Brian Horrocks did at the end of the 1950s. Boys' magazines, especially
the up-market full-colour paper *Eagle*, joined in projecting an essentially
exciting picture of the then recent war as both a great game and a good
cause. The generation of baby-boomers born in 1947–48 learned about
the Second World War from their parents, but they also saw a lot of
British war films as they came out. They could read dozens of books a
year about prisoner-of-war camps, combat and espionage (often in
special children's editions); and in boys' comics they really were offered
stereotypes. *Eagle*'s extended cartoon life of Winston Churchill, tellingly
entitled 'The Happy Warrior', retold the whole story of the Second
World War. Films could add more weight and a deeper impact to such
messages about what Studs Terkel later called 'the good war', and they
were usually more subtle; but the point is that films were reinforcing an
upbeat image of the war in popular culture, not creating it themselves.

In assessing these war films, we need to note the gap between the
guardians of film as art and responses of the public and the trade.
Reviews of war films in the *Monthly Film Bulletin*, in *Sight and Sound*
and in *Films and Filming*, were almost invariably lukewarm or negative,

and critics in the quality papers were also sometimes critical. War films were scarcely ever put forward for foreign film festivals, and were rarely mentioned when critics listed the best films of the previous year. There were common and increasingly insistent themes in these reviews by the mid-1950s: war films were 'old-fashioned' in highlighting a regrettable event and in a way no longer appropriate, they were socially conservative in a way that clashed with the demotic years of the Angry Young Men, and they encouraged irresponsible attitudes to future warfare. This last theme became more sharply articulated as CND increasingly high-lighted fear of the next war and carried many of the film-reviewing class with it.

In presenting such views, film magazines sometimes acknowledged uncomfortably that these movies might do well at the box-office because of an acknowledged public appetite for war-glorifying films. *Films and Filming* in 1956 offered sardonic 'congratulations to the publicists who made an average film, *The Dam Busters*, the most successful film of the year at the box office'. Two years later, it reported 'the surprising news' that *The Battle of the River Plate*, which it had unenthusiastically re-viewed, had proved the biggest box-office draw of 1957.

If we turn our attention to *Kinematograph Weekly*, the trade paper for managers and small proprietors of cinemas, we see a very different story: its reviewers generally welcomed war films, and almost invariably commented favourably on their box-office appeal. Its annual survey of box-office successes and failures by Josh Billings was based on returns from 4,000 cinema managers and is the best comparative evidence that we have. Its annual reports present a striking pattern. Almost all of the important war films of the 1950s were listed as doing exceptionally good business, eight being so listed in 1958 alone. War films were the first or second top-grossing British films in almost every year between 1955 and 1960: *The Dam Busters* was top in 1955, *Reach for the Sky* in 1956, *Bridge on the River Kwai* in 1958, and *Sink the Bismarck* in 1960. Only the *Doctor in the House* series did comparably well, while the early *Carry On* films were well behind in earning power – except, interestingly, *Carry On Sergeant*, with its military theme.

The genre faded rapidly after 1960, and died completely in the mid-1960s, challenged by comedians and satirists on television (*The Army Game*), radio (a classic POW episode of *Hancock's Half Hour*) and on the stage (for example in *Beyond the Fringe*). The latter, which eventually got the stamp of official approval when the Queen saw the show, contained a sketch called 'Aftermyth of War' in which Peter Cook as a stiff-upper-lipped RAF officer sent Jonathan Miller off to die on a crucial mission ('Goodbye, sir, or is it Au Revoir?' 'No, Perkins.'). The participants later remembered that this sketch occasionally caused outrage among older members of the audience, as when 'a gentleman of military bearing stood up, shook his fist and shouted "You young bounders don't know anything about it"'. But, as Roger Wilmot has pointed out, it offended only those 'who saw it as mocking those who lost their lives in the war, rather than the sentimentalised, stiff-upper-lip attitude of so many British films of the period'.[30]

There were plenty of films in the late 1940s about the aftermath of war, if not yet many that dealt directly with fighting, but in about 1950, when *The Wooden Horse* was released, the war itself became a popular topic. From then onwards, first prisoner-of-war films and soon afterwards combat films were at the heart of British filmmaking. In all about a hundred were made between 1946 and 1965. Apart from the crime films that have been ubiquitous in every generation, this was the largest genre within British cinema at the time – there were ten times as many war films as there were Ealing comedies, though Ealing has received *far* more attention in the literature.

Within the genre as a whole, however, bombing scarcely figured – less prominently indeed than in wartime films, when such titles as *Target for Tonight*, *One of Our Aircraft is Missing* and *The Way to the Stars* had all been important productions. This may well be explained by bombing's equivocal post-war reputation; in 1940–45, there was rather less squeamishness over the idea that Britain could 'dish it out' as well as 'take it'. There had been fighter films like *Angels One Five* (1952) and *Malta Story* (1953), and the air-sea rescue film *The Sea Shall Not Have Them* (1955), but the only film about bombing was the now mainly forgotten *Appointment in London* (1952). This was written and produced by a former bomber pilot, John Wooldridge, who had flown in Gibson's own 106 squadron, and although they had not been close he seems to have modelled Squadron Leader Tim Mason (Dirk Bogarde) on Gibson. When the film begins, Mason like Gibson is hoping to get to the end of a tour of duty and then rest from active operations. His pattern of behaviour (short temper, inability to sleep, fear of being *seen* to fear) is very close to the actual Guy Gibson of 1943, certainly closer to him than the 1955 film allowed Richard Todd to become. The film has a love interest – the girl interestingly being called Eve like Gibson's wife – and there are riotous scenes as the crews relax off-duty, but Mason is taken off duties because of his state of mind, only to see the squadron deteriorioate without his influence and a call back to duty for a major raid on a German secret weapons base. As with the dam-busting raid, but unlike the wartime bomber films, all of which concentrated entirely on surviving 'ordinary' operations, this feature film climaxes with a raid of special significance to the war effort. There is no claim about hitting small targets accurately, just a promise to flatten everything in the area of the special weapons establishment, and even then they do not manage to hit the central zone very well. Inevitably, the hero comes back successfully, keeps his 'appointment in London' (to collect a DFC), while a widow proudly collects the award for her dead husband and so confirms the acceptance of sacrifice. This summary may not do justice to a full-length film that has some good moments (notably the ragging of the signals and met officers during briefings that in other films can seem unconvincingly tame), but it indicates clearly enough that its main aim – to portray men under strain, even when on ordinary missions – was more ambitious but perhaps less welcome than the reassuring messages carried by *The Dam Busters*. It is, though, let down badly by a pedestrian script and by melodramatic acting and direction.

The prevalence of the war film genre in the 1950s, together with the fact that there had not yet been a particularly successful production on Bomber Command, therefore made it inevitable that a bestseller like *The Dam Busters* would become a film, that its pre-existing fame as a book (and indeed as an episode of the war itself) would make it a keenly awaited release, and that it would provide an opportunity to make a film with a very high profile.

TWO
Filming *The Dam Busters*

There seem to be no extant production files to shed light on the origins of *The Dam Busters* film, but much can be gathered from the memories of participants, memoirs, contemporary interviews, and especially from a series of articles by Laurence Thompson, published in the *News Chronicle* in June 1954 while filming was actually taking place. (A particular value of Thompson's pieces lies in the fact that he had access to several members of the production team and to the diary of Bill Whittaker, the production manager.) The overall budget for the film was reported by Whittaker to be £260,000, though when interviewed much later by Vincent Porter the casting director Robert Lennard recalled it as having been £200,000, so Whittaker's figure may have been somewhat inflated in an effort to present the film as a big project. It cost the production £130 an hour for the RAF crews of the Lancaster bombers, about 8 per cent of the total production budget. Other items mentioned were 15 per cent of the budget for the cost of artists and extras, 18 per cent for studio facilities, 10 per cent for sets, 7 per cent for 250,000 feet of film stock and laboratory services, 5.5 per cent for location costs, 3 per cent for 'story and script'; much of the rest must have gone to pay for the five specially adapted Lancasters. At one stage, cuts to the script had been imposed to keep the budget down but, in November 1953, these were restored and the decision taken to go ahead with a full-cost production; as Whittaker then noted, 'Michael Anderson to direct. Everything to be of top quality.' At a quarter of a million pounds this was a large budget for Britain in the 1950s; *The Colditz Story*, rather more typically, had cost £150,000, though by 1955 the biggest American films had budgets of a million pounds. Associated British strove to keep the budget for each production under £150,000, and it was clearly only the commitment of Robert Clark that allowed *The Dam Busters* a more generous sum.

The most crucial decisions were taken by Robert Clark, Associated

British's Director of Productions, as early as 1951–52. The first was to buy the rights to Brickhill's book, and the second that it would be bought so that Richard Todd, then in the middle of a seven-year contract with Associated British, could play Guy Gibson. The decision to buy the book was in no way surprising, except in the sense that Associated British's management was not known for its extravagance. It would have been expensive to acquire and process a bestseller like Brickhill's (the budget's £7,500 being shared between author and screenwriter), but in this case, eventual success at the box-office proved it a shrewd investment. It was Clark's custom to buy such literary properties for contract actors, though he had not recently been successful in finding suitable material for Todd, and it was his support that saw this expensive project through to completion.

Casting Richard Todd as the original basis for making the film was a less obvious choice. He was already a major figure in films, so far mainly in British ones though he had also been Walt Disney's *Robin Hood* and Darryl F. Zanuck was about to use him for *A Man Called Peter* (1954). He had already had considerable successes, including an Oscar nomination for *The Hasty Heart* (1949), and had played a string of heroic leading roles, including *Rob Roy* (1953); he would soon add Sir Walter Raleigh (*The Virgin Queen*, 1955). What he had not done so far was actually to make a modern war film – in the sense of a film about combat, since *The Hasty Heart* was concerned with a military hospital and the treatment of war casualties. Richard Todd became the epitome of the 1950s British war hero, in all arms of the service: for the Navy in *Yangtse Incident* (1957), for the Paras in *D Day, Sixth of June* (1956), *Danger Within* (1959) and *The Longest Day* (1962), and for the army in *The Long and the Short and the Tall* (1960); he turned down similar roles in *Ice Cold in Alex* and *The Guns of Navarone*. It comes therefore as something of shock to realize that his first such role came as late as 1954–55 in *The Dam Busters* – which was also his only time in RAF uniform until *Operation Crossbow* (1964) brought this phase of his acting life effectively to an end. It was, though, far from being a crude piece of studio casting, of the 'he's-under-contract-so-it-might-as-well-be-him' variety. Todd's trademarks as an actor were a certain inwardness (vividly so in the broken but stubborn spirit of his character in *The Hasty Heart*), unusual modesty in a leading film-actor (refusing, for example, to play himself as a heroic paratroop officer in *The Longest Day*), and a determination when in war films not to demean or trivialize the memory of the actual war and its casualties. Reviewing his career in

1958, and concluding that he was 'the only British star, based in Britain, who's an international film-selling name', *Picturegoer* explained his success as being due to the fact 'that he's an extraordinarily disciplined member of the all-too-often unstable acting profession'. Todd himself thought he had been lucky to become a star, for 'some of my biggest hits have been in films that were more important than the star, *The Dam Busters* and *Yangtse Incident* in particular'. Jack Cardiff, then directing him in *Intent to Kill*, thought that 'onscreen (and off, for that matter) he's a straightforward, nice, no nonsense kind of guy'.[1]

Casting Todd as Gibson would therefore ensure from the start that the squadron commander would be under- rather than over-played. Around his portrayal of Gibson, the whole film, as American critics despairingly pointed out, was steeped in 'characteristic British understatement'.

Three more early decisions by Robert Clark were of almost equal significance: the hiring of Bob Sherriff to write the script (others considered had included the Ealing veteran T. E. B. Clarke, C. S. Forester, Terence Rattigan and Emlyn Williams); Michael Anderson to direct the picture; and the casting of Michael Redgrave to co-star as Barnes Wallis (others considered included Laurence Olivier and, as Laurence Thompson put it, 'inevitably, Jack Hawkins').

R. C. Sherriff was the legendary dramatist whose play *Journey's End* (1928) had so vividly brought to the stage his own semi-autobiographical account of the trenches during the Great War. It had also incidentally transformed him from an impoverished insurance salesman into a rich man who could afford to follow his chosen vocation as a writer. Initially, he used his new wealth to buy himself an education at Oxford, where he rowed a good deal and read for a History degree. He was, however, soon lured to Hollywood by Sam Goldwyn, after an extraordinary conversation during which Goldwyn asked Sherriff how much he was being paid to write history essays for Oxford (presumably so that he could generously offer to double it), and was dumbfounded when Sherriff explained that it was actually he who was doing the paying. Initially, he intended only to interrupt his education, but it proved impossible to restart and he therefore became effectively a self-educated writer for the rest of his life.

From the 1930s on Sherriff produced a string of successful plays, most of which ran in the West End for several months, the most notable being *Home at Seven*, an effective screen version of which starred Ralph Richardson. But he was never able to replicate the runaway success of

Journey's End and was all too often therefore pigeonholed as a 'one-play writer'. His autobiography actually closes with an anecdote in which a lady he meets at a school speech day politely remarks, 'I *did* enjoy *Journey's End*. Why don't you write something else?' Sherriff, as a would-be playwright, had little to say in the book about his secondary writing career as a screenwriter, and most of what he did say was about the way in which the trade was plied in California, which he obviously found eccentric and largely inexplicable (if also very rewarding – he ran a Rolls-Royce on the proceeds). He offered only one throwaway line about *The Dam Busters* in his autobiography, though a good case can be made for it as his second-best work after *Journey's End*: 'I wrote the screenplay for *The Dam Busters*, which hit the bull's eye and took me on to the top of the world with the film studios; and from then on, in those golden years, I could write anything I wanted to.'[2]

By 1955, Sherriff's apprenticeship in films had been extensive, and, though jobbing screenwriters like him have rarely been given the recognition they deserve, his list of credits was impressive. Apart from helping to 'doctor' scripts like *Mrs Miniver* (1941), he had the writing credit for such classics as *The Invisible Man* (1933), *Goodbye Mr Chips* (1939), *The Four Feathers* (1939), *Lady Hamilton* (jointly with Walter Reisch, 1941), and *Odd Man Out* (1947). Looking back to what had made *Journey's End* a classic, it is not difficult to see where his talent for screenwriting really lay. He began the play by re-reading his own family letters from the front, to soak up atmosphere and language, and then imagined a group of officers like ones he had known. They are presented in the first scene with the knowledge of their own impending deaths in a great German attack, which will come three days later. This left room for no sub-plots, no glamour or colourful stage design, no female characters at all, no tension deriving from the plot (since the end is always inevitable), and no escape for his characters when the end comes. What makes the play so effective is what is left when all these factors have been excluded: truthfulness in character and dialogue. Sherriff himself later said that once the basic situation was clear, dictated by the historical events of 1918, his characters wrote their own words in his head; actors who perform the play have found his dialogue unusually easy to learn because it flows so naturally from situation and character. His relative failure as a playwright after *Journey's End* derived to a great extent from the fact that he was rarely able to think up plots good enough to produce the same easy flow of natural language. For films, there was no such problem, for he was usually assigned a dramatic story-line, again fixed in advance, an event from history or the adaptation of a novel. All he had to do was to turn a pre-determined plot into a filmable sequence of scenes and then ensure that the actors had credible words to utter, exactly what he did so well. Sherriff could do this best if the story's characters were mostly men, and especially if they were also situated in the all-male environment of a school or a military unit. In *The Four Feathers* or *Goodbye Mr Chips*, the few women characters seem to have no life between their lines; in *The Dam Busters*, the only real female role, Mrs Wallis, is stereotypically domesticated and motherly, and is generally knitting. Sherriff's own life was mainly spent in the male company of school, army, rowing and cricket clubs, and in the war service of 1914–18 which he regarded as his life's most fulfilling moment. He chose to call his autobiography *No Leading Lady* (which surely implies rather more than a factual comment on *Journey's End*), and when he died in 1975, *The Times* included in his obituary the then telling phrase, 'he never married'.

There is one other point to stress in assessing Sherriff's input. As a writer, he was always very conscious of his Britishness and of British ways of acting and speaking; it is no accident that he was a stalwart of the Hollywood cricket club. At exactly the moment when sound films were about to sweep all before them, in 1928, Sherriff captured in *Journey's End* the way in which a certain type of British officer and gentleman spoke and behaved. He then carried these manners and forms of expression into his screenplays, was much imitated in doing so, and saw them develop into clichés of cinematic Englishness. When in *Journey's End* the authorial voice, Lieutenant Osborne, is told that he is being sent on a suicidal raid, he does not complain, and when another officer says insensitively that it is all 'a damned nuisance' (another type of British understatement), Osborne merely replies 'It is rather'. When in *The Dam Busters* Guy Gibson is asked to do another mission even though his tour of duty should be over, and then to fly lower than is safe, he loyally but without bravado agrees. When Gibson himself says to Wallis of the failure of the prototype bombs to bounce, 'It's the devil, isn't it?', Wallis responds, 'It is rather'. Sherriff's pen and Todd's acting would naturally choose the same tone of voice. Both were themselves war veterans who were modest about their experiences but had a sense of obligation to comrades who had not survived; both had rather con-servative political and social attitudes, and both at one time considered making careers as Conservative politicians (as indeed did Guy Gibson). And, like both Gibson and Todd, Sherriff was a dog-lover with a weakness for fast cars.

All this made *The Dam Busters* a perfect subject for a Sherriff screenplay. The plot was pre-determined by the 1943 events, the characterizations of the major figures had been provided by Paul Brickhill, but this could be supplemented anyway by Gibson's autobiography and by interviewing 617 squadron's survivors. Sherriff's role would be to turn the book into acted scenes and filmed sequences. This was in itself not difficult, since only a hundred pages of the book dealt with the raid, and since Brickhill had already written some dialogue into his prose account. The filmscript contains much dialogue taken straight from the book (some of it from Gibson's book, filtered through Brickhill's). There are, though, also occasions when differences are introduced by Sherriff for deliberate effect. When Gibson and Barnes Wallis first meet, for example, an important moment in the story, Brickhill has a third party (the test-pilot Summers) present throughout, contributing strong personal opinions to the conversation; Sherriff has Summers introduce Gibson to Barnes at the start but then leave them, so allowing a strong personal rapport to be established between the film's two stars. The film would also have 'no leading lady', and little love interest, but its characterization would depend rather on establishing with credibility the ways in which the young airmen of Britain and its empire talked to each other within a formal command structure in wartime. This Sherriff could conjure up – and his success in picking up actual RAF lingo remains impressive. Michael Anderson had read Brickhill's book when first assigned to the film, but had never met the author, while the actors, many of whom had also read the book, barely even met Sherriff, so linear was the process by which their script evolved, and so complete was that process before they arrived for filming.

But if Sherriff was, on reflection, almost an obvious choice, the selection of Michael Anderson to direct the film was certainly not. Indeed, when first told about the choice of such an unknown director for this big job, Richard Todd was irritated rather than reassured, attributing it to the familiar parsimony of Associated British's Scottish management. (Dinner with Anderson at the Café Royal won him over, and personally they then got on famously, going on to make two other pictures together, both war films.) Anderson, though, had had a formidable apprenticeship to some of the biggest names in the classic decade of British cinema and was known to professionals in the industry by the early 1950s as the best assistant director around, a man ready for the next move forward. He had gone from school at the age of fifteen straight to work in the studios, initially as a tea-boy though always wanting to direct, and had worked his way up with such luminaries as Anthony Asquith (*French without Tears*), David Lean (*In Which We Serve* – for which he also had to act in one scene, after Noël Coward fired an actor who arrived late on set, without having learned his lines) and Carol Reed. As he moved from third assistant director into the higher but still invisible ranks of the trade, he had greater opportunities to show what he could do, and gained the reputation of being able to work with some of the industry's most difficult men, with Peter Ustinov for example on *Private Angelo* (which he co-directed in 1949, aged only twenty-nine), and with the actor Robert Newton on *Waterfront* (1950, his first solo credit as a director). *Picturegoer* headlined an appreciation of Anderson in 1958 with the words, 'He gets the best out of stars'.[3]

Michael Anderson had made five more films since 1950, none of them now much remembered, but was clearly ready for a bigger production and a higher level of public and critical notice. *The Dam Busters* certainly provided that, though before it was released he had already directed an effective screen version of Orwell's *Nineteen Eighty-Four* (also starring Michael Redgrave). He went on in the next few years to direct the blockbuster *Around the World in Eighty Days* and *Yangtse Incident* (both 1956), *Chase a Crooked Shadow* (1958), *The Naked Edge* (1961), *Operation Crossbow* (1964) and *The Quiller Memorandum* (1968). Thereafter his career rather stalled, perhaps in part because of his move to Canada, leaving his British reputation behind; *The Shoes of the Fisherman* (1968) was a major project, but he took over only when the director Anthony Asquith died, and *Conduct Unbecoming* (1975) was strongly cast but never quite escaped the confines of the play on which it was based. Taken as a whole, Anderson's collective output made him one of Britain's major post-war film directors, and one of the few ever to maintain a lengthy career in Hollywood, but he has never quite received the credit he deserves in the literature on British cinema. This may derive partly from the way in which Mike Todd managed as producer to grab most of the plaudits for *Around the World in Eighty Days*, Anderson's first truly international success, though it won Anderson an Academy Award nomination. But more important was surely his association with a type of well-made film that went out of fashion when he was still in his forties. We might say that critical acclaim from the 1960s onwards would lie more with the radical approaches of a Lindsay Anderson than with the well-made films of a Michael Anderson.

Screenplays like Sherriff's and film-acting like Richard Todd's would also go out of fashion in the 1960s, but their convergence with Anderson in *The Dam Busters* was a great asset to the production at a time when all three were on top form and in tune with public taste. All three shared a commitment to straightforward stories and to truthful presentations of actual events. When Sherriff was asked in 1939, 'You ever been mixed up in politics?' (which of course he had), a question bound up with his desire for an American visa so that he could propagandize for Britain in Hollywood, he responded that he had 'never written a word with a smell of politics in it. I just write plain, straightforward stories that can't do any harm to anyone.' Likewise Todd welcomed *Yangtse Incident* when offered the part because 'the subject sounded to me just the kind of thing I would enjoy: like *The Dam Busters* an authentic true action story which British movie-makers did so well'.[4] Interviewed in due course about *The Dam Busters*, Anderson responded that the thing that had attracted him to the project was the story and the fact that it was all true.

This is not to suggest that Anderson was a stereotypical director who always made the same type of film, for that would be far from the truth. He was, for example, already telling interviewers in 1955 that he was fascinated by the creative possibilities of colour and widescreen technologies (so foreshadowing his work on *Around the World in Eighty Days*), but that he had decided on a black-and-white format and a traditional screen-ratio for *The Dam Busters* because he wanted to achieve the documentary feel of a film of the early 1940s (and indeed to allow the incorporation of actual 1943 footage too). Anderson was interested in the British documentary tradition, fused into feature filmmaking in wartime but apparently lost from view again by the mid-1950s. One of his aims in *The Dam Busters* was to re-create that marriage of styles, so generating a film that had both the feel of documentary truth and sufficient professional polish to hold an audience's attention for a couple of hours. To judge from the reviews even of tough-minded critics who did not particularly like war films, he succeeded in this self-imposed task. It was also the explanation of this approach that won over Richard Todd from scepticism to approval of his assignment as director.

Sherriff, Anderson and Todd had further common ground in their personal determination to make the film as accurate as possible; later, Associated British's PR men sold the film as the 'true story' of a great wartime exploit. Brickhill had already interviewed as many original witnesses as he could find, and had clearly been given a great deal of help in writing his book by Mickey Martin (the Australian flyer who commanded 617 squadron shortly after Gibson's departure), Charles

1. *The historical adviser (Group Captain Whitworth) explains a detail of the raid on the dams to Michael Anderson (left) and Richard Todd.*

Whitworth (who had commanded at RAF Scampton in 1943) and Barnes Wallis. Sherriff nevertheless went over much of the ground again when adapting the book for the film, and some changes in dialogue with no apparent dramatic purpose probably derive from the changing recollections of survivors or the finding of different witnesses. Whittaker's diary for March 1952, for example, records Sherriff describing a visit to Barnes Wallis, where the scientist had set up in his garden 'the catapult, water tub etc. with which he did his original experiments. Mr. Wallis proudly conducted us to them and said, "it's just as it was at the time. Now I'll show you how it works." It didn't.' (It did later, though, when un-perished rubber was found for Wallis's catapult, and this duly became the opening scene of the film.) The art director Bob Jones shared the same dogged commitment to absolute accuracy, getting newspapers, posters, service regulations and even cigarette packets reprinted so as to be 'right' for 1943. Jones's days spent ferreting around on the Scampton airfield produced design ideas for aircrew bedrooms and he had a bonus when he stumbled accidentally across 1943's wartime operations room and copied it for the cavernous studio set used in the film for the raid sequences.[5]

Anderson made similar contacts and encouraged his lead actors to do so as well, searching for ways of making truthful portrayals of both the living and the dead. Interviewed by Trevor Heelas in 1967, Anderson remembered that 'the war films that I have directed mostly have been based on truth, and I find that I can, by means of research and probing, come up with something that is near the truth'.[6]

In casting the role of Mickey Martin (still alive and shortly to conclude his career as Air Marshal Sir Harold Martin, KCB, DSO, DFC, AFC) he interviewed scores of actors to get both the persona and the moustache just 'right', before settling on Bill Kerr. As he later recalled: 'This was a luxury. I'm sure the audience wouldn't be aware of the fact. But it was something I felt was a responsibility of mine towards the people who were in the planes.' Bill Kerr's own recollection is of being summoned by his agent from a duck-shoot in Western Australia and being greeted by Michael Anderson when he arrived at Elstree with the words, 'Gentlemen, Mickey Martin has just entered the room.' He also ruefully remembers that despite his resemblance to Martin he had to spend an hour and a half in make-up on each filming day, during which he acquired a moustache, a red wig and chocks behind the ears. George Baker, as David Maltby in what would be only his second film (though beginning a five-year contract with ABPC), may also have owed his casting to his looks. He was in 1954 so strikingly similar in appearance to how Maltby himself had appeared in 1943 that the technical adviser Charles Whitworth conflated appearance with reality and eerily kept calling him 'Dave'. Robert Shaw, cast as Flight Sergeant Pulford at the suggestion of Michael Redgrave, also owed the part to his close resemblance to the original.

Richard Todd talked not only with Sherriff and Anderson while preparing to play Guy Gibson, but also with Mickey Martin and others of 617 squadron, with Barnes Wallis, and with Gibson's father. He went one further than the others by talking even to Gibson's scoutmaster, so discovering that Gibson always wore a small boy-scout badge on a band at his wrist. This Todd duly did during filming, though it is barely visible and never remarked on, just as he also adopted Gibson's way of standing, and his habit of wearing a captured German 'Mae West' lifejacket in the flying scenes (also never commented on). In this general aim of replicating in detail the real Gibson, Todd was clearly very successful. Having seen a pre-release copy of the film, Gibson's father (who had earlier expressed reservations about the making of the film at all, being 'afraid of departure from the facts, over-dramatisation, and the introduction of sentimentality in the story') wrote to say that 'in Richard Todd you have chosen an actor who is, to my mind, ideally cast for the part of Guy ... and I am personally deeply grateful to him for his understanding interpretation of the part'. When the film was released, the *News Chronicle* sent its air correspondent to see it as well as its film critic, and former RAF man Ronald Walker reported that 'the impersonations are uncanny. Richard Todd is extraordinarily like the late Wing Commander Guy Gibson VC as I remember him.'[7]

Why exactly was it important to get such 'invisible' details as the scout badge right? In part, says Richard Todd, this was in keeping with Anderson's overall directive to secure documentary accuracy, but it was also a case of 'getting it right' as a matter of principle, because actual events were being re-created on film. On the same principle, Todd would later dismiss the cherry-red paratrooper's beret provided by a studio's wardrobe department for *Danger Within* and send home for his own weatherbeaten, pale-pink wartime paratrooper's beret to use instead, even though on a black-and-white film it would be almost impossible to see the difference. It just had to be 'right'.

Michael Redgrave took a rather different approach. When cast as the scientist Barnes Wallis he agreed to meet Wallis himself, but told him bluntly that he would make no attempt to mimic him. 'Quite right,' said Wallis. 'Your problem is not to imitate a person but to create him.' Redgrave did, though, hit it off with Wallis, for when they met and the slim, diminutive Wallis realized that he was being played by an actor well over six feet tall and heavily built, he burst out laughing; as Redgrave recalled, 'we "clicked" at once'.[8]

Redgrave indeed welcomed the part because it gave him a rare opportunity as an actor to create an onscreen persona that had absolutely none of himself in it, and later remembered it as the most interesting filming he had done for many years. But in truth he had little to do with the choice of the part. As Corin Redgrave shows, Redgrave was in dire financial straits in 1954, the consequence of three classical seasons at Stratford and the Old Vic, during which he had played Shylock, Mark Antony, Hamlet, King Lear, Prospero *and* Hotspur. As this indicates, he was then at the height of his powers as a stage actor and this was what mattered to him. Within a month of finishing work on *The Dam Busters* he told a BFI summer school: 'I am primarily a stage actor and ... my aversion to being referred to as "the film star" amounts to nausea.'[9] But

2. *Barnes Wallis (left) with Michael Redgrave.*

in 1954, in order to effect a rescue of his finances, he had placed himself
entirely in the hands of his agent, accepting whatever work was on offer
(though it still took some persuasion from Michael Anderson actually to
take on Wallis). This meant six films in succession, some with scripts of
no particular value, and some like gold-dust, such as the part of Wallis
– though, oddly, he played senior RAF officers in two of the six,
the deservedly forgotten *The Night My Number Came Up* and the
rather better *The Sea Shall Not Have Them*. There was no denying his
catholicity of taste since his film debut in Hitchcock's *The Lady Vanishes*,
for, in addition to air marshals, he had recently starred as John Worthing
in Anthony Asquith's *The Importance of Being Earnest* (1952), and his
next screen role was singing and dancing through *Oh ... Rosalinda!* an
adaptation of *Die Fledermaus*. If anything in his previous career showed
him to be so right for the part of Wallis, it was playing Andrew Crocker-
Harris in Terence Rattigan's *The Browning Version* (1950), another character older than himself, undervalued and tortured by self-doubt.

But if Redgrave did not want to avail himself of direct evidence from
Wallis in preparing to play the part, he nevertheless became fascinated
by the life of the scientist, telling an interviewer that he had secured

permission to visit Wallis's workshops whenever he wished. When not needed on set, he was often there, quietly watching the scientists at work, observing their body-language and absorbing something of their patterns of behaviour. In its way, this generic research was as important as Todd talking to the relatives, and it allowed Redgrave to give a strongly individualized performance in *The Dam Busters*, the best thing he did on screen. His early biographer Richard Findlater thought that in his Wallis,

> bent-shouldered, gentle-mannered, stubbornly-civilian, single-minded fanaticism was combined with warm-hearted friendliness; one could see the immense patience of the *worker* ... and the childlike simplicity of the man; and it was another of Redgrave's achievements that he distinguished the artist in science from the artist in literature or acting, while illustrating Wallis's own kind of creative truth.[10]

In short, he had created on screen 'not a stock type but a real person'. This reflection in turn sheds some light on the problem that Todd had in re-creating Gibson, leading one or two reviewers to contrast them much in Redgrave's favour. Todd too was seeking to create a person rather than a type, but the legendary Gibson did not easily respond to such treatment, for as Patrick Gibbs wrote of Gibson's autobiography, Gibson *was* 'less a personality than a type ... It is as if a composite character, the eternal pilot, had written this story, an illusion increased inevitably by the prodigious nature of the career.'[11]

Beyond the casting of Todd and Redgrave, and the director's personal wish to get Mickey Martin so 'right', the casting of the other forty speaking roles in *The Dam Busters* cannot have been difficult, for Sherriff's script had determined that none would have much chance to attract our attention. Individuals who crop up in only one or two scenes were chosen from experienced film actors so as to give even subsidiary roles a weighty feel – Charles Carson and Raymond Huntley being good examples of this. Basil Sydney specialized in playing the sort of senior-officer roles that he now got in Bomber Harris, and the other older actors with noticeable RAF parts (Patrick Barr, Ernest Clark and Derek Farr) were well matched to their roles and nicely contrasted with each other. The bulk of the cast, however (seventeen out of twenty-eight named roles in the film), playing the young men of 617 squadron, were actors who would necessarily be unknown to the public because they had to be young enough to carry conviction as aircrew on active service. John Fraser (Flight Lieutenant 'Hoppy' Hopgood), indeed, was still young enough to have had two pop records released with success during the 1950s. The flying part of the cast, however, included several actors who had parts in similar films around this time: George Baker in *The Ship That Died of Shame*, Nigel Stock and Bill Kerr in *Appointment in London*. There were also many who would move on to major careers in the future – even if we leave aside Bill Kerr who for a generation was the British people's favourite Australian in BBC radio's *Hancock's Half Hour*. These included Brewster Mason who went on to play Falstaff and other major roles at Stratford, George Baker who was also at Stratford for many seasons before finding wider fame with television's *I Claudius* and *Inspector Wexford*, and Robert Shaw who went on to a major international film career.

FILMING HISTORY

There was no question of rushing this film into production – it was, after all, because of its name and content, a topic that could wait until ABPC was good and ready. Their purchase of the Brickhill book ensured that nobody else would get there first, as did the active co-operation of the RAF, without which nobody could make such a film. A full screenplay from Sherriff was ready by autumn 1952, but no filming took place for eighteen months, and there was then another year between the end of filming and the film's release. The first of these intervals allowed for the research described above, for extensive technical preparations, and for the script to be refined. Bill Whittaker's diary confirms that these were all essentially matters of detail, for the first full draft, considered at a script conference in August 1952, 'met with universal approval, but suggestions and discussion took place on a large number of detailed points', including the acceptability of individual lines and the exact way in which certain scenes might be staged for the cameras. Laurence Thompson, reviewing the script in June 1954, concluded that it was 'a good script ... though a little reverent, an Albert Memorial rather than a transcription of life'. He also recorded Wallis's delphic comment when asked how accurate it was: 'No one scene is the truth, but the whole thing adds up to the truth.'

The interval before starting filming allowed time for copies of the script to be sent all over the world so that survivors, witnesses and next of kin who could not be interviewed because of distance could also have their views considered. From Melbourne came back the unfortunate response of Flight Lieutenant Jack Leggo: 'I have received the copy of the script sent to my father, and I learn that you have written to my father on the assumption that I was dead. I am very glad to say that this is not the case.' Another veteran sent back the minatory advice, 'Do it right, or not at all. Extract the digit, Mr. Clark, and make a dam (sic) good film. If you shoot the line as per Errol Flynn you will be haunted by some very tough types, and you never know what you might find in your beer one night.'

Often responses were in direct conflict, so confirming that Sherriff had got it just about right. While Sir Arthur Harris complained that he had been made into an ogre, another veteran of Bomber Command thought he had been made 'far too human'. In this case at least ABC made amendments, the scene in which Harris first meets Wallis being rewritten by the studio's Walter Mycroft to make Harris less unsympathetic and Wallis less of an 'outsider' to the RAF establishment. Some responses, like the recollections of Gibson's batman, had to be dismissed as unreliable (among other things, when he visited during filming he claimed to recognize Gibson's dog which had been killed in 1943), but others provided the basis for changing a few words here, or a nuance there, as successive drafts of the script were produced. In key areas, though, the script never departed from strategic decisions made at early script conferences, when Sherriff had produced an outline but not a word of actual dialogue. It was decided as early as March 1952 to endorse his view that 'the story ... should be told simply and naturally, with no recourse to tricks of any kind. It was also agreed that there should be no attempt to introduce a feminine influence.'

There was extensive contact with the RAF itself in this preparatory period, from as early as October 1951 (Brickhill's book had been published in September). The RAF provided access to thousands of feet of 1940s film, some of it captured from Germany in 1945, but was unable to secure permission for the ABPC film to be shot over the real Mohne and Eder dams (which meant that far more models would have to be used). The Germans were not likely to be co-operative over the 'glorification of a gruesome event' and some German papers were particularly upset when ABPC staged the film's première in the same month in which Germany regained its post-war sovereignty. The real benefit of the Air Ministry's help came in opening up the facilities of the RAF itself, the use of airfields and provision of trained aircrew, and overcoming vested interests within the government that wanted to stop or to limit the project on security grounds. This all took a long time, and led to filming repeatedly being postponed, but it also greatly enhanced the eventual film.

Preparation for filming had also included work on models and special effects, some of which were shown to the actors as they assembled for filming in the spring of 1954, and greatly impressed them. Barnes Wallis, shown the model of the Mohne dam that would be blown up for the film's climactic moment, was heard to mutter, 'Good God! You must have put in every pine tree.' Lengthy preparation also meant that the actors had an entirely finished script to deal with; there would be no need for the hasty overnight rewrites, speed-learning of lines and hurried readjustments in rehearsal that characterized the shooting of many films.

Location shooting began in April 1954, with Trafalgar Point on the northern (Lincolnshire) corner of the Wash standing in for Kent's Reculver sands, while the team lived in Skegness. (In Skegness, Todd had the sort of experience that can only come on location but which only a modest actor would have recounted to anyone else: when a teenage girl sought his autograph and confessed to having seen *Rob Roy* seventeen times and *The Sword and the Rose* thirteen times, he asked innocently what she did for a living: 'Oh, I'm an usherette in a local cinema.') From there the cast and crew moved on to Lincoln for filming at the RAF bases of Scampton and Hemswell. Scampton, the actual base of 617 squadron, was the main location, and it was here that the cast saw the film's five specially modified Lancaster bombers arrive to join the team. Richard Todd recalled

> droning specks in the distance, gradually increasing their sound to a shattering roar as they passed low overhead and in perfect wing-tip to wing-tip V-formation ... [Everyone] turned excited eyes to the sky. The black war planes wheeled several times as they 'beat-up' the airfield within feet of the hangar roofs, obviously showing off to the cheering waving crowd below. Then, scorning the runway, they landed still in V-formation on the grass. What a display! What a moment![12]

The skill demonstrated by the RAF pilots in flying low, both for this spectacular arrival and for the film, indicates once again how essential was the backing of the RAF. (This was especially the case when it became clear that bombers flying at 60 feet did not *look* dangerously low when photographed; the 1954 pilots thus had to fly even lower than the bombers of 1943 had done, in order to create the desired effect, and on one occasion this led to a plane's landing wheels brushing the top of a hangar.) Since there were only five Lancasters available, that is the maximum number seen in any one shot. Fortunately, most of the training and all of the raid sequences required formations of three bombers or fewer, though there must have been much painting and repainting of identifying marks on the fuselages of these five planes in order for them to appear to be nineteen. When more bombers had to be seen in ground sequences, Lancasters are in the foreground, and rather similar Lincoln bombers (still then in service and indistinguishable to the amateur eye at a distance) fill in at the back.

The film's aircrews spent hours in and around the bombers at Scampton, getting the feel of the planes they were supposed to be able to fly, in some cases receiving extensive flying lessons (on the ground) from RAF technical instructors, so that they would seem to know what they were doing, and filming exterior shots of squadron members assembling for briefings, dispersing, lounging around in anticipation of the raid, and the final departure and return. When not needed for all this, the Lancasters were off with a camera plane to film aerial sequences over lakes in South Wales, Essex, the Lake District and Derbyshire. Given the length and complexity of the aerial sequences in the film, this location shooting must have continued long after the exterior scenes involving actors were in the can. With a finished script, and with a director who went straight into filming rather than conducting acting rehearsals off the set first, location shooting was brisk and was completed early. Erwin Hillier, cinematographer on the film, noted soon afterwards that Anderson 'shoots what he wants to shoot. He can save the studio thirty per cent of costs that way.'[13] Anderson's detailed preparation, and the quiet authority on the set which the actors remember, emerged particularly in scenes involving large numbers of actors. George Baker remembers, for example, that once Richard Todd had delivered his briefing speech for the raid for the basic 'take', there was no need for endless repetitions because the director had worked out exactly how he wanted reaction shots to be set up, and they moved briskly on from one to the next. Michael Anderson's own memory of this is of his need constantly to explain to his actors exactly what was going on during scenes where they were being filmed without dialogue. He achieved a remarkable narrative lucidity as a result of this.

It was not easy to film on the base while its normal life went on: on one occasion six perfectly good takes were ruined as Canberra bombers landed one after the other, anticipating history by a few years. Crowds of airmen gathered to watch filming, and the RAF's other ranks demanded the use of their mess (in 1943 and in the film the briefing room) as soon as meal breaks commenced. Nor was it easy to tell who was who, so an order of the day went out: 'Personnel will have noticed a great many queer characters about. Don't pay any attention to them. They're only actors.' Several actors in uniform found themselves saluted by groundstaff as if they were the real thing, while Group Captain Whitworth was heard to roar, 'You salute me. I'm *not* an actor.' A visiting air vice marshal remarked brightly to Anderson, 'I knew you film people were here. I saw another Air Marshal strolling about the hangars and [with horrified face] he was *chewing gum!*' The actors had been given use of the officers' mess for the duration of the filming, but 'Flight Sergeant' Robert Shaw was then denied admission on the grounds that he was not an officer. After an embarrassing row, the actor-NCOs were also allowed in, but only if they *removed* their uniform jackets, surely a mess rule unique in the history of armed-forces etiquette?

The only real hiatus in that phase of the filming was bizarre, and related to Gibson's dog, an RAF dog on loan to the production and personally handled by the dog-loving Todd. There was no doubting the affection that had rapidly built up between them, and Todd recalls the dog as being an object lesson in a fellow-actor, quick on the uptake and hardly ever requiring a retake. (Just once, when he was required to wait for a knock on the door in Gibson's bedroom before jumping off the bed and running over to see who was going to enter, he could not easily be persuaded to await the knock – after all, he knew what was going to happen, so why wait?) But, when 'Nigger' was supposed to stroll with 'Gibson' through a group of RAF men as they gathered for a briefing just outside the Scampton HQ building, he positively refused to move and could not even be dragged past the spot on a leash. It transpired that under the grass at just this point lay the body of the real 'Nigger', buried eleven years earlier and usually commemorated by a grave-marker, temporarily removed during the filming. Had the actor-dog somehow sensed something of the presence of the dog that he was playing in the film? It was decided to leave him out of the scene. 'Nigger' was the actual name of Gibson's dog, of course, and the filmmakers now stuck to it in the interests of accuracy, but it also gives some indication of the mores of 1950s Britain; such a name would have been unthinkable in the United States at that time. For the American version of the film, the dog became 'Trigger', despite its overtones of the Western, presumably because it was the easiest word to dub on to the soundtrack. By the end of the century, Britain had belatedly caught up. When ITV showed the film in 1999 the network was apparently 'inundated with complaints', as a result of which the soundtrack was edited to remove the offending word. When it was next shown in June 2001, ITV was criticized instead by anti-censorship campaigners.[14]

Any film on location that encounters no difficulty greater than the need to exclude an animal from a scene in which its presence is not commented on has not encountered serious problems. After a break allowed by the early finish of the location shooting, the cast reassembled in mid-May at Elstree for studio work, all the indoor scenes and those shot in and from the cockpit of the bombers. A simulated Lancaster fuselage had been built, mounted on a large ball and socket joint so that it could be rocked in any direction. Now, through the hottest days of the year until mid-July, the actors sweated it out under lights and wearing full kit, flying-helmets and masks. Richard Todd's inability to hit it off with Robert Shaw, who was morose and not perhaps content with his supporting role, cannot have made being cooped up with him for eight-hour days any the easier. He remembers this, though, because it was so *un*characteristic of the mood during filming. More often there was a real sense of teamwork and of an important film being made, confirmed on a regular basis as the 'rushes' were viewed. This is not entirely sur-prising. The older members of the cast, like Todd himself, Nigel Stock, Brewster Mason and Derek Farr, had all themselves served in the forces during the war, and had a clear memory of service life. Bill Kerr had wanted to join the RAAF but could not pass the maths exam and so spent his war in the army, but had a close friend who had been shot down over Holland. The younger members like George Baker and John Fraser (both born in 1931) were just the age for the parts they played in 1954 and brought natural high spirits and enthusiasm to them. When filming ended on schedule in mid-July 1954, there was a real end-of-term feeling, and regret that such a harmonious cast would now be dispersed. There was also a strong sense among them that they had made a film that would prove to be quite out of the ordinary.

THREE
The Film: *The Dam Busters*

THE INVENTION

The opening titles of *The Dam Busters* offer fourteen frames of information, accompanied by two musical themes that will recur throughout the film. The very first title (indicating that this is an Associated British Picture Corporation production) is accompanied by the fugato which Eric Coates had used to build up tension before the arrival of his big tune. As the music switches to a short and even more portentous bridge passage, we see the names of the film's two stars, Richard Todd and Michael Redgrave, billed in parallel as co-stars, and with their two film characters each given his full name, rank and decorations – hence indicating before a line has been spoken the film's commitment to detail. As the big tune finally arrives, the title of the film appears, with credits to both Brickhill's and Gibson's books. The march tune, re-edited to the necessary length, underpins all the succeeding credits for the cast and technical crew but, as Michael Anderson's name appears as the director the music switches to a different tune, an upwardly reaching, yearning motif that is not from Coates's 'Dam Busters' March' at all. That new music continues under the film's final opening title, which acknowledges assistance in the making of the film from the Royal Air Force, A. V. Roe Limited, survivors of 617 squadron, and from the next of kin of flyers who did not survive; once again, this pitches a strong claim to the film's authenticity.

As we read that final title, the music dies down from the martial to the pastoral, and the film itself begins with the caption 'April 1942' set against a cloudy sky. The camera pans down to a country lane, a car with an exceedingly careful driver who gives the correct hand signal in the deserted lane as he pulls across into the drive of a substantial house. His white hair, build and avuncularity of expression, together with his bag, proclaim him to be a family doctor, much like Alastair Sim in *Waterloo Road*. The actual house where this scene was filmed was to be

Harold Wilson's country retreat in the 1970s, and he took delight in confusing new visitors to Great Missenden by asking them if they thought they had seen it before.

The relaxed, seven-minute opening scene tells us much that we need to know about the plot to come, the character traits of a central personality and of the government, and the essential technical problem to be solved over the next two hours. The doctor (Charles Carson) has come ostensibly to visit Barnes Wallis's sick daughter, but really because Wallis's wife (Ursula Jeans) believes Wallis to be in need of a rest. However, hearing noises from the terrace, the doctor enters that way, and therefore encounters Wallis himself (Michael Redgrave), who is conducting with his children some bizarre experiment involving catapulting marbles at a tin-bath filled with water, and noting where they land. To the children, this is all a huge game, but the young Elizabeth's reluctance to go to bed, because 'I've got to help Daddy play marbles', also pre-figures people's scepticism about Wallis's ideas. The doctor confirms that 'he seems to be having a fine, old game out there'.

Mrs Wallis, however, introduces some seriousness; Barnes has been out in the rain since 5 a.m. conducting his experiment, failing to come in for tea and wearing wet shoes (when he finally comes in he agrees to take off the shoes, but does not remember to do so). His urgency derives from the necessity to have something ready for a committee meeting tomorrow. Wallis eventually comes in, only to be delayed further by the need to set up the blackout (night having just fallen with amazing speed, given that this is the home counties, nowhere near the equator). In doing this, he and the doctor return to the terrace, drawn by the drone of bomber engines overhead. This sounds like another big raid on Germany, but, says Wallace, it will be ineffective because Bomber Command is trying to kill a giant by aiming pea-shooters at his limbs, rather than firing a bullet through the heart. This is a dangerous moment, even a potentially subversive one, for the line just quoted might well invite the question of why the war needed to last for two more years after the Dambusters had apparently shot Germany through the heart, while Wallis's supporting argument about the ineffectiveness of existing bomber tactics ('Well, you know what happened when they tried to wipe out London') no doubt evoked suitably patriotic memories of the Blitz, but undermines claims of what Bomber Command did in 1943–45.

Unsurprisingly, the doctor offers no such scepticism and, returning to the house – Mrs Wallis having retreated to make tea – he and Wallis get to scientific men's talk. Wallis's idea for an 'earthquake bomb' is now to be directed at the three great dams that provide water and electricity for the Ruhr munitions industries, and with the aid of maps and drawings the doctor (and therefore the audience too) is inducted into understanding the booms which make it necessary to bounce a bomb across these reservoirs and then explode it at the base of the dam wall. Having heard the problems, the doctor concludes sadly that it cannot be done. This gives Wallis the opportunity to tell us that he has now worked out how to do it, but is barely ready to prove his idea before tomorrow's scientific committee. The doctor, innocent in the ways of Whitehall, asks why he does not work it all out and then get them to set up another committee. The reply hints at a lifetime of difficulties with bureaucrats, but the chime of a clock brings the conversation to an end anyway, the doctor having to return to his surgery. Before leaving, he carries out his promise and urges Wallis to get away at least for an Easter break, which prompts Wallis to ask if the doctor believes that he's going crazy – many people think so. The doctor of course politely resists such an idea and the scene closes with a dissolve into an establishing shot of traffic in Whitehall.

That opening scene has already hinted at official obstruction (though even Wallis agrees that 'this part's easy compared with what's coming'), at people's suspicions of his mental balance, and at his own serious-minded but evident obsession with one big idea. When the doctor, about to tell him to take a rest, asks, 'Will you promise me something?', the reply is not an easy but insincere 'Of course', but a delayed, troubled, 'If I can'. The job will come first, whatever the consequences. The scene also offers any number of petty reminders of wartime life and its atmosphere which audiences of 1955 would most certainly not have missed: the blackout curtains, white paint on the car, and the doctor's polite refusal, until Wallis insists, that he take a little rationed sugar in his tea.

Whitehall traffic prepares us for the crucial meeting of scientific advisers, but the scene begins in the anteroom, where Wallis confronts the committee's distinguished chairman, Dr David Pye (Stanley Van Beers). He briefly explains his dilemma, a new idea not yet sufficiently developed to allow committee discussion, and asks Pye to get them to give him more time. Once inside, the camera frames the committee table so as to put Pye at the very centre, dominating the sceptical discussion of Wallis's request, a discussion in which only one other member is supportive. Pye's authority is not challenged, however, and Wallis is given not only extra time but also access to additional research facilities at Harmondsworth. (Model dams had been built there at the Road Research Laboratory, and its workers were christened locally 'the dam blasters' – so much for national security.) The committee members raise their hands in support with obvious reluctance, confirming early in the film the negative way in which civilian officialdom responds to ideas.

Mention of Harmondsworth and its model dams has prepared us for a dissolve straight to the place itself – a technique that Sherriff uses a good deal in this part of the screenplay, dialogue that facilitates smooth progression between scenes. Continuity is also provided by the Pye committee's arrival at Harmondsworth to inspect Wallis's work. Wallis has therefore to explain to the scientists and to us what will take place, the explosion of two miniature bombs. One is larger but further away from the dam, the second smaller but attached to the wall. The first explosion duly makes little impact, the second (despite Wallis's 'this ought to get our feet wet') catching out the scientists and drenching one or two. This breaching of the model dam, shot from low-down on the dry side, so that even what we know to be a model seems substantial, is accompanied by a short burst of music, the first on the soundtrack for six minutes and an effect that will be replicated when the real dams are breached. This is a nice moment, giving the soaked sceptics a miniature come-uppance for which the audience has been yearning, but it does not deter them. Wallis is now even more seriously barracked on the need to find a way of delivering the bomb, and of exploding it in the right place. This cross-examination sequence has Wallis framed in isolation, but once again Pye intervenes as the wise authority figure, stopping the bickering, suggesting that Wallis move on to the ship-testing tanks at the National Physical Laboratory at Teddington, and offering a final word of encouragement to the inventor: 'I think you're on to something.' Though Michael Anderson brings Wallis and his tormentors together into the frame with Pye before their departure, Pye visibly healing the breach in his committee, he also allows the camera to linger on Wallis after they have gone: Redgrave, shot from a low angle and dominating the frame completely, is cleaning and polishing his glasses, but his face is a rich mixture of confidence, satisfaction at another hurdle sur-mounted, and concern about what is to come. Pye, by 1955 Sir David Pye FRS, is the only major scientist named in the film, though both Sir Henry Tizard and Sir Patrick Blackett also played their part as helpful (if sometimes sceptical) scientists while Wallis's project developed. Pye has to stand for them all, a reasonable elision that reduces what would otherwise be a confusing multiplicity of names and faces. And the real

Pye did indeed help Wallis by shielding him from less sympathetic members of his committee.

Once again, the cut to a large water-tank at Teddington (filmed at the actual NPL laboratory) has been prepared for. We see a catapulted golf-ball fail whatever test it is that Wallis is now attempting, and his weary instruction to change one of the experiment's variables yet again. Cutting to the outside of the building, the Pye committee is welcomed by the NPL's director (Raymond Huntley) – a wonderfully smooth, duplicitous characterization that received honourable mentions in reviews, though he is actually onscreen for only about a minute. (This character too is unnamed, and is a good deal less helpful to Wallis than was the actual director of the NPL.) As they walk towards the tank, we learn that Wallis has already been there for five months, frequently forgetting to go home at night and remembering lunch only about once a week. Wallis's obsession (and with an idea which the director clearly regards as barking mad) is causing all sorts of problems, for others have experiments waiting to use the tank too, a reasonable point undermined by the supercilious way he defends it: 'Look, couldn't you find him some quiet duck pond in the country? Some place where he can shoot things up and down without being a nuisance to other people?' Once inside, the committee is greeted distractedly by Wallis, and – with fine dramatic timing – his experiment now goes perfectly, the golf-ball obediently skimming the water just like a pebble on a duck pond and hitting the end with a satisfying rap before sinking to the bottom. And to prove that it was not a fluke, he does it a second time. Shots of the golf-ball flying and bouncing are rapidly edited to convey high speed, but the reaction shots among the observers are a picture in themselves, quiet satisfaction from Wallis, bewilderment giving way to pleasure from Pye, scarcely concealed disappointment from the others. The NPL's director is barely even ruffled when Wallis disarmingly asks if he had thought him to be going mad ('Oh, my dear fellow, that's the last thing...' – it was indeed the last thing he had said on the soundtrack). For, says Wallis helpfully, 'There's a very thin dividing line between inspiration and obsession, so that sometimes it's very hard to know which side you're really on.' The director does not, however, miss the chance to get Wallis to confirm that he will be off the premises by the weekend. Generally, though, the scene ends in triumph, with Pye confirming (despite continued reluctance in the ranks) that they will be putting in a positive report: 'After that, it's a matter for the Ministry of Aircraft Production.'

The MAP had a heroic reputation in the war years, launched in May

3. *Wallis (Michael Redgrave) is congratulated by the committee of scientists while the NPL director (Raymond Huntley) and Dr Pye (Stanley Van Beers, right) look on.*

1940 under Lord Beaverbrook's dynamic leadership, and achieving small administrative miracles in cutting red tape, removing logjams in production, and delivering battle-saving Spitfires and Hurricanes by the summer. The verbal link forwards from Pye's remark at Teddington to the next scene of the film, visibly set in a bureaucrat's office, does all that is needed to explain the next location, but it would hardly have prepared 1955's audience for the mood of the scene. This is the first of three short scenes at the Ministry, in each of which Wallis is confronted by the same unnamed civil servant, a finely observed characterization by Hugh Manning of all the worst traits of cinematic Whitehall – but much like the portrayal of the civil service in Bomber Harris's memoirs. In order to avoid giving offence to any one man, or indeed to have his claims refuted from specific experience, Brickhill had noted of 'two high officials' who seemed 'irritatingly cautious' that 'they shall be nameless'. In the film, too, the obstructors are also all nameless.

Instead of rushing to cut red tape, this smooth-faced public servant lectures the inventor on the wearisome number of people competing for

MAP's scarce resources of money, factory space and skilled labour. He responds to Wallis's despairing argument that this makes it all the more crucial to develop ideas such as his which could shorten the war, with the sharp rejoinder that they do indeed do all they can to develop 'weapons of known value', but that that is hardly comparable to ideas that are so 'revolutionary...I might also say fantastic ones'. His only positive response is 'possibly next year, when things may be easier?' but it is crystal clear that this particular official will never authorize Wallis's idea, at any time or anywhere. He is, however, pleasingly checkmated by Wallis's past successes. Wallis has asked for the use of one Wellington bomber, so that a prototype bouncing-bomb can be tried out. What, he is asked patronizingly, could the official possibly say to his masters to persuade them to release such a valuable resource as a Wellington? Well, perhaps, responds Wallis shyly, 'if you told them that I designed it, do you think that might help?' After about eighteen minutes, this is the film's first joke, and once again a source of audience satisfaction as official pompousness is pleasurably punctured. A quick cut to a Wellington bomber taking off leaves us in no doubt of the effectiveness of Wallis's thrust, but while laughing at the joke we may well miss the real moral, which is that if Wallis had not already been known as a successful inventor and designer, then his brilliant idea would *never* have got past the first stage of bureaucratic obstruction.

The Wellington bomber does, however, take off, its crew being Wallis as bomb-aimer, and as pilot 'Mutt' Summers, a nice RAF-sounding familiar for Captain Joseph Summers, OBE (Patrick Barr), the Vickers test-pilot who had also been the first man to fly a Spitfire, and portrayed with considerably less attention to accuracy by David Niven in Leslie Howard's *The First of the Few* (1942). We see them in the cockpit, much as Guy Gibson and his flight engineer will be filmed later in the movie, making a good-humoured bet as to whether their experimental bomb will bounce. Having nervously confirmed that speed and altitude are correct, Wallis eventually (the delay, from the expression in his eyes, allowing for a wish or a prayer) presses the trigger. Viewing some of that wartime RAF footage, we see a bomb bounce several times on the water, while Wallis whoops with joy, Summers fumbles unavailingly for a coin with which to pay his bet, and the soundtrack again provides a musical celebration (it is once again more than five minutes since any music has been heard).

The switchback of the emotions in this part of the film continues with another short scene in which that MAP official again deadbats

Wallis's request for action. 'Personally,' he purrs, 'I'd like to see you go straight ahead, but if anything the position is more difficult today than it was when I saw you last month.' When Wallis insists on the value of his new bomb to the war effort, he hides behind a corporate decision: 'I can only pass on to you the decision of the Ministry.' His only real suggestion is in itself a damning indictment of Whitehall, for he recommends Wallis to talk to a person of influence who could by-pass the official channels (himself). And this is pointless anyway, for Wallis has already seen, tried to see, or sat for hours outside the offices of, all the well-connected people suggested. 'In that case,' the official concludes without apparent regret, 'I think for the present that you've done everything you can', clearly considering the matter closed.

It is worth pausing here to reflect on the politics of these scenes, with their entirely negative portrayal of the civil service. It is inconceivable that such a lampoon would have occurred in films of the 1940s (except when they showed *pre*-war events, as in *The First of the Few*, where Leslie Howard's R. J. Mitchell encounters much the same obstruction from civil servants when trying to persuade them to adopt his Spitfire). For the most part, the nation's wartime administrators had been portrayed as effective planners, partly because of the shot in the arm given to the civil service by the wartime importation of clever outsiders. It was, after all, because of a consensus that government knew what it was doing that there was public support for a massive extension of state power in the post-war world, in nationalization, the welfare state and the National Health Service. It was in 1947 that the Labour Minister Douglas Jay attracted so much attention by arguing that 'in the case of nutrition and health, just as in the case of education, the gentleman from Whitehall really does know better what is good for people than the people know themselves'. By the end of the 1940s, however, this was no longer a view on which there was a political consensus; the Conservatives squeezed back into power in 1951 with the slogan 'Set the People Free' (from government controls), proceeding to wind down rationing, planning and other types of state intervention.

The relevance of all of this to wartime bombing can be indicated by reference once again to Harris's memoirs. Not only did he blame Whitehall obstruction for preventing him from winning the war without the need for D-Day and the land campaign that followed, but he also added, just after a passage on the dams raid had been cited as evidence of what the RAF could have done with proper support, a veritable tirade on the theme: 'After thirty years experience of working under the dead hand of the Civil Service, I am persuaded that the progressive multiplication of government departments and controls, operated by civil servants who are themselves multiplying fast, is leading the country to catastrophe, complete and perhaps irreparable.'[1]

This view had not gained wide acceptance when published in 1947, but eight years later the climate of opinion was more welcoming, while, only another eight years after *The Dam Busters*, Enoch Powell would offer the argument that government was in fact uniquely bad at planning, that almost everything that it did turned out badly, and that the market choices of individuals were the only sure judge, because (reversing Douglas Jay) ordinary people invariably knew more about what they wanted than governments ever could. Such a view, of course, became dominant in the later part of the century.

That broad cultural shift against the credibility of government and the effectiveness of the civil service was widely reflected in the cinema, and because of the size of cinema audiences in the 1950s, films must at least have reinforced the trend. Consider, as an example, the contrasting ways in which a wartime film, *Tawny Pipit* (1943), and a film of a decade later, *Conflict of Wings* (1954), each explore the basis on which environmental issues should be related to national defence. In wartime, the local community unites to defend the nesting site of a rare bird, saving it from the depredations of the army, but is persuaded by a wise government that both of these needs must be accommodated. In *Conflict of Wings*, the community rallies to protect its local bird life against the plan to set up a firing range, the government's claims for the needs of national defence are brushed aside, and the local people's judgement is upheld by the film against 'the gentleman from Whitehall'. Much the same can be seen in Ealing comedies, as for example in *Passport to Pimlico* (1949), where Basil Radford and Naunton Wayne turn their famous 'Charters and Caldicott' double act into a Whitehall farce, concerned as civil servants only to drink tea, go home on time and pass the buck. In *The Winslow Boy* (1948), even a service department, the Admiralty, comes under attack for high-handed lack of regard for the citizen's rights, while standing up against such dictation is presented as a peculiarly British virtue. In the industry's sustained denigration of the civil service, *The Dam Busters* fits in nicely, then, but because it had such a large audience it was no doubt more than usually influential, and because it retrospectively invalidated even the civil servants' finest hour in wartime, it goes rather further than most films in a negative direction.

Wallis does take the MAP civil servant's advice, albeit not in the way intended, for we next see him persuading Summers to help him take his idea straight to Bomber Command, trading on the fact that Summers knows Harris personally. Summers is at first sceptical, knowing personally not only Harris but his temper, and betraying his own lack of conviction in Wallis's bomb by reminding him that all sorts of cranks go to Harris with ingenious but impractical ideas. It is decided (in fact by Wallis, Summers effectively dissociating himself with, 'Don't blame me if he throws us out of the window') to take a chance on Harris, but it is the only chance that remains. The film therefore cuts straight to a cardboard label which tells us we are in Harris's headquarters.

Harris (Basil Sydney) duly lives up to his reputation as a forceful personality, greeting Summers with 'Hello, Mutt', but sharply telling 'Mr Wallis' that he's read the report and needs no lectures on the value of breaching those dams if it could be done. (What Harris actually said was, 'What the hell do you damned inventors want? My boys' lives are too precious to be thrown away by you', a sentiment which the film reassigns later to Wallis himself.) Wallis, relatively ineffectual in many scenes of the film, now stands his ground staunchly, telling Harris that his scheme is not like other clever wheezes, since it *works*, and he has film to prove it. A discreet veil is drawn over the failure of the administrative machine to take the necessary action (Harris: 'If you've proved the thing, why wasn't it taken up?' Wallis: 'I don't know'), and Harris is urged to watch just five minutes of film and then decide for himself. There is a tense moment of delay while Harris decides whether to give way in this battle of wills, and we sense that everything hangs on this powerful man's answer, but the silence is terminated by a brisk decision to watch the film, a quick march to the projection room, and a responsible order rapped over his shoulder: the projectionist should be sent away and his staff officer show the film (actually the same Saundby who in 1955 complained that the film was inaccurate), for 'If this thing's as good as you say it is, there's no point in letting everybody know'.

We – the cinema audience – do not follow them into the projection room, and so, apart from the fragment of film we saw during the test, we still have not seen the bouncing-bomb – this is being reserved for more effective use later. We do expect, though, that the long period of frustration is over, but the film has one last switchback ride for us. It now cuts without explanation to Wallis's house, easily recognizable and anyway inhabited by Mrs Wallis and her knitting. Responding to his wife's eager questioning, Wallis tells us of Harris, 'Oh, he was all right', but goes on to drop the bombshell that Vickers have passed on to Wallis

4. *Wallis (Michael Redgrave) is comforted by his wife (Ursula Jeans)*
after it seems that his research will be called off.

a reprimand from Whitehall for wasting too many busy people's time
(this was based on actual events, for plenty of people at Vickers were
also pretty fed up with Wallis's obsessions by this stage). He has therefore resigned from the firm altogether. Suggesting that even she does
not quite share his faith in the bouncing-bomb, Mrs Wallis asks, 'But
surely this doesn't affect your other work?' In a unique moment of
domestic closeness, Wallis sits on the arm of her chair and bares his
soul: 'Sweetheart, when you believe in a thing as much I've believed in
this, there really isn't any other work until you've seen it through.' His
use of the past tense is itself rather shocking, for even the Churchillian
fortitude that kept him going in Harris's office now seems to have been
defeated. He has resigned on impulse, giving no thought to the future
(or indeed to how to provide for his wife and children) and now muses
that he could probably get a job teaching somewhere, and that in the
meantime there is a long list of home maintenance and gardening tasks
that have been neglected. The mention of gardening brings into the
soundtrack a brief musical reprise of the pastoral theme of the film's

opening, while the reference to gardening is a veritable Sherriff trademark: all the good chaps in his plays and screenplays from *Journey's End* onwards have a weakness for making rockeries or planting broad beans, a pianissimo echo of the English rural myth.

Inconsequentially, Mrs Wallis remembers that the Ministry had rung just before Wallis returned, and must see him urgently in the morning. Wallis at first refuses to go merely to be reprimanded again, but when his wife quietly urges that he *should* go, just in case, he agrees, but only to tell MAP precisely what he thinks of them. Domestic closeness has continued through the scene, a nice touch being Mrs Wallis's lightly brushing something off her husband's lapel as she urges him to do his duty (possibly some white hair powder that Redgrave used to age himself for the part of Wallis). This is Mrs Wallis's final appearance and the last named female character to appear in the film at all, though it still has a hundred minutes to go. The only women's voices from now on will be anonymous WRAFs offering bacon and eggs or cups of cocoa, and there will be no further scene set in a civilian dwelling of any kind. From now on, the war is exclusively men's business and predominantly for the warriors, and the only love interest is between Guy Gibson and his dog. It is absolutely impossible that a war film made during the war itself would have so marginalized women, as this film now did in 1955, for in 1939–45 there was a drive to celebrate all parts of the community in a collaborative 'People's War'. Interestingly, it appears that women in 1955 responded to their marginalization by coming to see war films in lesser numbers than men.

We are therefore primed to expect another conflict when Wallis arrives for the third time at the Ministry of Aircraft Production, beginning the conversation at cross purposes with the ever-smiling official and preparing to give as good as he gets. It soon transpires, however, that he's been summoned for a quite different purpose, and the official tells him pompously that, 'What I'm telling you now is official': the go-ahead has been given. How? Churchill himself, presumably on the advice of Bomber Harris, has authorized the raid to go ahead, 'right away. The Prime Minister is enthusiastic about it.' Thus, part at least of the administrative myth of the war is being replayed for the film, for Churchill has demanded 'action this day' and the bureaucrats have leapt into action. The film's conservative message is being reinforced by the uniformed warriors Harris and Churchill saving the day when the pin-striped bureaucrats let everyone down. There is in fact no evidence at all that Churchill intervened (except perhaps to approve the final go-ahead when the Navy wanted the raid postponed, since he was in Washington when the Chiefs of Staff made that decision, and he is unlikely to have left them in ignorance of his views), and considerable evidence that his scientific adviser Lord Cherwell was like Harris dead against the idea. Brickhill, who greatly admired Churchill but not Cherwell, noted outrageously that Cherwell (the former Professor Lindemann) was 'German-born'.

MAP's civil servant even has the nerve now to lecture Wallis about the urgency of the task, pointing out that only two months remain before the water level in the dams will fall, a fact he got from Wallis's report in the first place. 'These civil servants!', we can hardly forbear from muttering. The scene – and the first section of the film – ends, though, not on a note of either vindictiveness or triumphalism but with sober realism. It will be hard enough to create and train a squadron in the time, but can Wallis do his part in getting the bombs ready? Sinking into a chair, borne down by the responsibility, he can only answer, with a complete absence of both the heroic and the theatrical, 'Well, I'll ... I'll do my best.' He is clearly thinking, to quote his remark of almost a year ago, that what has happened so far is nothing compared to the difficulties to come.

THE TRAINING

Harris is the only direct link between parts one and two of the film; the next scene begins as he is concluding a briefing with his senior bombing commanders with the demand for a 'real hit at Essen' in that night's raid. One of the commanders, Air Vice Marshal the Hon. Ralph Cochrane (Ernest Clark), is kept back when the others disperse and asked about Wallis's idea. Though it sounds 'far-fetched', he responds, 'Personally, I think it can be done'. Harris responds more sceptically, 'I hope you're right', but orders Cochrane to create a new squadron of experienced flyers ('Some of those keen youngsters won't mind doing an extra one'). Does Harris have anyone in mind to lead the squadron? 'Yes, Gibson.' The story's combat hero is thus first mentioned half an hour into the film, and his name (the last word in the scene) links forwards to a bomber landing on an RAF airfield, obviously Gibson himself descending like a *deus ex machina* to do the impossible deed.

Gibson (Richard Todd) first appears in his cockpit, weary but relieved to have got safely to the end of a 'tour' of thirty missions, and confirming with a little technical jargon that he and his engineer Flight Sergeant Pulford (Robert Shaw) are careful and sensible flyers ('Rad shutters

5. *Gibson (Richard Todd) with 'Nigger'.*

auto', that sort of thing, impressing us precisely because we haven't a clue what it means). As the crew clamber down from their Lancaster, we see Todd's batman Crosby (Harold Goodwin) holding a black labrador on a leash, and as Gibson himself appears at the hatch the dog strains forward, encouraged by Gibson with 'Come on, Nigger', is let off the leash and greets Gibson with great affection. As it rolls on its back to have its tummy rubbed, Gibson tells Nigger, with considerable dramatic irony, 'Well, you won't have to wait for me for a long, long time. We're going on holiday, down to Cornwall … ' His bomb-aimer 'Spam' Spafford (Nigel Stock) urges Gibson in broad 'Strine' to 'Get a move on, skipper, or you'll miss the bus!' (Bill Kerr derived considerable amusement from Stock's accent, Stock's casting owing more to his facial similarity to Spafford than to his facility with the Australian accent.) Breezy service lingo continues as the scene shifts to the mess, where Gibson's crew plan to see a London show before splitting up for leave, noting that you can usually get into theatres (except in the stalls, 'because of the Americans' – a sly reference back to the 'over-paid, over-sexed and over here' joke about Americans in wartime Britain). Gibson, the commander but also one of the boys, will form one of the party, but he now receives the order to report to Group headquarters on the following morning, a request that produces a puzzled 'Right'.

A car duly drives up to an imposing building and Todd emerges, leaving his dog in the car (he is virtually never without the dog except when in a bomber or visiting a senior officer), and receives a sentry's salute. We are at (the real) Group HQ in Grantham, and Gibson enters Cochrane's office, saluting smartly. When asked if he would mind taking on one more mission he loyally accepts, though he can be told no more than that it involves low flying at night. They are joined by Group Captain Whitworth (Derek Farr). Whitworth, greeting Gibson warmly ('Oh, yes, we're old friends'), commands the base at RAF Scampton where 617 squadron will be located, and has orders to help Gibson get things going. Cochrane's parting advice is that a new squadron of experienced flyers will attract a lot of attention, so there must therefore be very tight security. Gibson and Whitworth leave to begin the task by picking their men.

A personnel officer provides photographs and service records, and we are rapidly given an introduction to faces that will figure in 617 squadron, so rapidly that little can be taken in. The patterns, though, are clear enough, and of real interest. The first to be named are two more Australians, a New Zealander, and the American Joe McCarthy ('Oh … the glorious blond. He used to be a Coney Island beach-guard'). Whitworth urges Gibson not to forget about the English, and several other names and faces flash across the soundtrack and the screen, notably 'Dinghy' Young (whom Whitworth had taught to fly in the Oxford University air squadron) and Henry Maudslay. Young had been a rowing blue, while Maudslay was 'a darn good athlete too. He's a miler.' We are being subtly reminded that these are all men from the elite, both physically and socially, but the geographical spread is also worth consideration. It is indeed the English who will figure in 617 squadron (hardly a Welsh or a Scottish accent to be heard, nor indeed one from the East End, the West Midlands or the North) together with those from the empire. The dutiful mention of Joe McCarthy is never followed up, and he plays such a small role in the film that he does not even get into the thirty-eight acting credits. It is to be 'part of our Empire's story', rather than a celebration either of the diversity of the United Kingdom or of the Atlantic alliance. This may well have been all to do with accuracy of detail – a third of bomber aircrews were indeed from the Dominions and 617 squadron was just like that – but a film would not have been made in this way if produced ten years earlier. In 1945, a film about the

Dambusters would surely have included a prominent role for an American actor, and it would certainly have had a Scots character part for either John Laurie or Gordon Jackson. As it is, the only Scots voice on the soundtrack is a single ground technician at Scampton, rather like all those Scottish engineers who run the ships' boiler-rooms in movies about the empire ('Can you give me fifteen knots, Mac?' 'Aye, I can that, Captain.')

In each case, the selection of personnel has been about the pilots, and when briefing for the raid itself takes place it is by the pilots' names that the planes are identified. This is Gibson's world-view, drawn from his autobiography via Paul Brickhill, but it was also something about which Michael Anderson was entirely unrepentant. Interviewed in 1967 by the BBC, he responded:

> Well, I think it's part of our national way of life to some extent, isn't it? I mean we've always had below decks and above decks, or there was below stairs and above stairs ... There are always these distinctive classes and I think they are as much in film as they are in real life ... I mean this is the way we remember our own days in the forces, most of us.[2]

That last point is significant, and not difficult to accept, for the hatred of military hierarchy when they experienced it (most of them, inevitably, at the bottom of the heap, and without the benefit of inspiring leaders such as Richard Todd offered in films) was one reason that fuelled British servicemen's swing to the left in the war years, but in those years no filmmaker would ever have portrayed the armed forces in such a hierarchical way. Then, they strove relentlessly to show that it was otherwise, but by 1955 a conservative message was back in vogue.

The film is, though, demonstrably incorrect in giving the impression that all the pilots of the new squadron would be decorated veterans. 617 squadron had more than its share of such men, and this did help to give it such a distinctive mood and quality, but it also had its share of those who only just made the grade (some of those who flew the dams raid had completed fewer than ten missions over Germany), and not a few that Gibson sent back to their squadrons as soon as he'd looked them over. Such a truth would undermine the special status given to 617 squadron by the film, even when still on the drawing board, but it was again a misconception drawn from Brickhill, probably from the faulty reminiscences of his witnesses. In due course, the film's concentration on only the first wave of bombers during the dams raid enables it not to portray some rather less distinguished flying in the rear columns, one of whose pilots flew into the sea, two of whom probably collided with power cables, and several of whom got hopelessly lost somewhere over Holland. One reason that 617 squadron did not hit enough of its targets and do greater damage was that too many of its pilots were not yet good enough when low flying at night. Nor does the film mention Bomber Command's amazingly confident statement, when instructing Groups to give up their best pilots to the new squadron, that 'the operation against the dam will not, it is thought, prove particularly dangerous'.

Asked by Whitworth what he himself will do for a crew, Gibson replies cheerily that it's easy enough to get a crew, and his old one deserves a rest: 'They've had a hard time. Must be sick of the sight of me by now.' Back at base, Gibson encounters one of his crew, Flight Lieutenant Trevor-Roper (Brewster Mason), and tells him that he cannot join them for dinner and a show because he has a new job. Will he break the news to the others? Gibson now tells his batman that he need not hurry with the packing, but not to unpack either, since, 'We're moving to Scampton'. So, no leave for Aircraftman Crosby, apparently, though Gibson does considerately tell him to take the chance to go and get his dinner, the other ranks of course having their 'dinner' in the middle of the day, officers in the evening. As he completes packing personal things, Trevor-Roper and fellow crew-member the Canadian Flight Lieutenant Taerum (Brian Nissen) enter. Is Gibson going to fly in his new job? 'Of course I'm going to fly.' Well, the crew have 'held a committee meeting', and 'it's the general opinion that it's not going to be safe to let you fly about with a lot of new people who don't know how crazy you are', so his old crew must give up their leave and follow him to the new job. Visibly pleased, and once he is facing away from them smiling broadly, Gibson responds in the same bantering tone, 'Well, if that's what you want to do, all right. But I think you're the crazy ones, the whole bunch of you.' Before Gibson meets the new squadron, we have had a timely reminder of his ability to inspire loyalty in his existing team – all couched in the half-humorous language expected from British cinema's service types when an emotional corner has to be negotiated. When, after the dams raid, Gibson was forcibly removed from active service, his crew stayed on in 617 squadron and four of the six were killed together in autumn 1943. Gibson, who had just met Taerum's parents while propagandizing in Canada, now had to send them his condolences.

An exterior shot of an airfield and its 1930s-style headquarters building introduces us to RAF Scampton; the bubbling conversation, faces recognizable from those personnel office photographs and plenty of colonial accents make it clear that the squadron has now assembled. Another tiny detail of absolute correctness has Martin with a soft drink in this scene though surrounded by beer-drinkers – Anderson had discovered that the real Martin did not drink alcohol. A brief moment of not very convincing lower-class humour (always Sherriff's weakness) now intervenes, as two mess waiters review rumours they have heard ('There's eleven DFCs already ... They say it's a plot to kidnap 'itler'), but Sherriff also smuggles a tribute to Gibson into the waiters' prattle: 'Oy! Here's Gibson. He's done a hundred and seventy-three sorties already.' Gibson and Whitworth circulate among the recruits, many of whom they greet as old friends, and single lines provide the chance to identify others: the mustachioed Australian Flight Lieutenant Mickey Martin (Bill Kerr) is told, 'I wanted you for this. You're the low low-flying expert.' 'Low flying? Fine.' The light-heartedness of these young men is brought out both by their acceptance of the new job without having the faintest idea what it is, and by one of them standing 'Nigger' a pint of beer. Apparently the real dog was so keen on beer that he crept up on anyone lounging with his tankard hanging over the arm of an armchair and helped himself.

Asked when their bombers will arrive, Gibson replies that it will be tomorrow, a dialogue link into the next scene, which shows three Lancasters landing on the airfield – the film's other real stars have arrived. Moving to the briefing hall, Gibson finds his men now standing respectfully and fully engaged in what he has to tell (plenty of reaction shots linking speaker and audience in a collusive act). What he can actually tell them, though, is still not much: security will be vital, low-level flying must be practised day and night, and 'if it comes off it will have results which may do quite a bit to shorten this war'. That latter claim, made before Gibson himself knows the target, is repeated several times during the training sequences, in the same large but unspecific terms, so reminding us that this is all of real strategic importance. It's never contradicted as the film concludes, so we are clearly intended to accept it as the film's view of what happened in 1943.

Suiting action to the word, we immediately see six shots of bombers flying low over lakes, with (as in all such sequences) a good deal of engine noise on the soundtrack. This sequence then dissolves into a pivotal moment, as Wallis and Gibson first meet in Wallis's office. There is embarrassment stemming from the fact that Gibson has still not been informed about their target, while Wallis is not allowed to tell him (he nervously scans the list of those with security clearance and finds that

Gibson is not one of them, then at the end of the scene quickly scans it again, as if somehow Gibson's name might by then have materialized). They hit it off well, considering the difference of age and background, and Wallis is touched that Gibson would like to understand some of the science involved in his new invention. The real point of the scene, though, is that Gibson is shown the film of the testing of the bouncing-bomb, and we now see both the film itself and his open-mouthed amazement. Back in Wallis's office, he asks if a 5-ton bomb can really bounce on water like a ping-pong ball, and is told by Wallis, with commendable understatement, that, 'It's been hard to persuade some people that it will.' Asking Wallis if he had actually thought all this up himself, and being told, 'Well, I think I may say that I invented it', Gibson bursts out with, 'Well, I think it's terrific'. The scene catalogues the technical problems still to be surmounted: flying below the level at which an altimeter works and getting speed and distance exactly right for dropping the bomb. Confronted by these, Gibson does not offer a gung-ho promise, merely that 'it's hard to say offhand' whether his men can do it. This corresponds to his memoirs' account of his state of mind as he began training for a well-nigh impossible task, metaphorically kicking himself for volunteering.

Enlightenment is now at hand, for his return to Scampton is followed by Cochrane producing three large models of the dams to be attacked, and hence information about the purpose of it all. There is also a reminder of the increased urgency because of all those earlier delays: the raids will be effective only if carried out when water levels be-hind the dams are high, and this means that there are only five weeks before the raid has either to be carried out or postponed for at least half a year. Since, as Cochrane assures us, the raid 'will bring the Ruhr steel industry to a standstill', urgency is everything. He tells Gibson to go down to Reculver in Kent, where Wallis's new bomb is to be tested. This we also want to see.

The new scene starts a sequence in which bomb tests at Reculver alternate with the squadron's mastering of the technical difficulties of flying low and dropping bombs dead on target. The first test is a disaster for which we have not been prepared, the bomb shattering as soon as it hits the water, the Ministry officials grimly wearing 'I told you so' expressions, and one actually saying out loud, 'I said all along it wouldn't work'. Wallis's isolation is emphasized by his eccentric behaviour, taking off his shoes and socks and wading out into the sands as the tide recedes, so as to feel about with his toes for fragments of the bomb – a sequence

6. *Wallis (Michael Redgrave) explains progress on the bomb tests to Gibson (Richard Todd) and his bombing officer Bob Hay (Basil Appleby).*

accompanied by a lonely-sounding minor-key version of the film's pastoral theme.

The second test is even worse, not least since its failure is witnessed by more men from the Ministry, three carloads of whom leave without a single word to Wallis (whose own reaction has been to take an involuntary step backwards and utter a flat, 'Oh, my God!') Harris is also present this time, preparing himself mentally for the decision to abandon the entire project, and giving Wallis one more week to get it right. Joined by the pipe-smoking Gibson who has watched the test from further off, Wallis responds to the remark, 'It's the devil, isn't it', with the tightly buttoned, 'It is, rather'.

By this time, the problem of low flying has been solved by Gibson himself. Pausing in London to take in a show, on the way back from the first Reculver test, he sits (in the stalls, actually) in what seems to be the London Coliseum theatre, and notices that the singer on stage is illuminated by follow-spots from left and right, the beams of which move with her across the stage, changing shape as the distances from the lanterns vary. This produces a pensive look, and less interest in the glamour on stage than he had evinced at the start of the scene (drawing a pitying look from the officer in the next seat). Gibson has realized that two lights, fixed to the underside of an aircraft at correct angles, would always come together on the water when the plane was at the planned altitude. We see this being tested over a lake, as the bomb-aimer's voiceover intones, 'Up a bit ... Down a bit', but never actually says, 'Back a bit' (for which Bill Kerr was mercilessly lampooned thereafter by his Australian friends). The squadron can now celebrate a success in the mess. When Whitworth asks sceptically whether they do not mind carrying lights into a raid (so making it easier to get shot down), Martin breezily remarks that it would be better than landing up 'in the drink'. Confident in this, Gibson is even able to reassure Wallis after the second Reculver test that they can fly at sixty feet if necessary – 'Oh, we'll do it alright.' By now the relationship between Wallis and Gibson is well established, despite the generation gap: the RAF men call Wallis 'the old man' and to Gibson he calls them 'your boys'.

The story of Gibson inventing the low-flying trick while at the theatre is, alas, entirely fictitious, for it was a scientist at the despised Ministry of Aircraft Production who came up with the idea of using two lamps. Sherriff probably picked up the idea of theatre spotlights from Brickhill's account of Mickey Martin's reaction when told what the Ministry was recommending: 'I could have told you that. Last night Terry Taerum and I went to see the ENSA show and when the girl was doing her striptease, there were these two spotlights shining on her and the idea crossed my mind then, and I was going to tell you.' The effect of giving the credit to Gibson is to reinforce his centrality to the film's story – and gratuitously to hit the Ministry below the belt. Harris also gets off lightly here: when he heard of the proposed use of spotlights, he minuted, 'as I always thought, this weapon is barmy ... I will not have aircraft flying about with spotlights on in defended areas ... Get some of these lunatics controlled, and if possible locked up!' He presumably forgot to mention any of this when he complained that the filmscript made him seem unduly unsympathetic.

Before the climax of this segment of the film, we have a rare moment of light relief. As the bombers practise their low flying at night, an exasperated North-country poultry-farmer (Laurence Naismith) writes to the press to denounce 'idiotic joy-riding' by pilots, since the noise they produce (vibrations that rattle the crockery on his table) is making his hens produce eggs prematurely: 'They drop off the perches and mess up the floor … This means a serious loss both to me and the country.' (When the actual bomb was tested at Chesil Beach, there were complaints of the disturbance caused to nesting swans at nearby Abbotsbury – was Sherriff thinking of this, or of similar complaints from Essex farmers that their cows were refusing milk after low flying over a reservoir near Colchester? And after the real raid, members of 617 squadron tried unavailingly to hoax *The Times* with an ornithologist's letter of protest that the raid had not been delayed until after the breeding season for the Mohne lake's rare – actually, non-existent – swans.) The film's farmer would not be reassured to know that when the plane that deafened his hens gets back to Scampton, its crew finds part of a tree wrapped round the Lancaster's wheel, so low had they been flying; this news is received with high-spirited jocularity. 617 squadron did indeed come back with foliage wrapped around the Lancasters' wheels and radiators during this dangerous training

But time is running out, and the final bomb-test is set up carefully to screw up the tension. We the audience have already been told by Harris that this is Wallis's last chance, and we know too that the water-level and the moon will not be correct beyond the following week. The test is preceded by a nervous little scene at Manston airfield, with Wallis telling Summers, 'It's now or never, Mutt', and Summers responding, 'You pray for me, and I'll pray for you'. The Ministry men are meanwhile waiting for Wallis, bemoaning their wasted time and openly looking forward to his failure. Their drive to Reculver, Wallis later tells Gibson, makes him feel 'as if I was being driven out to my own execution'. Gibson, very positively, tells Wallis that they have solved the low-flying problem, and that he must make a wish under the new moon, 'our moon. It's going to be a lucky one.' Wallis responds with a heartfelt, 'I hope so … Oh, I do hope so', and is clearly thinking beyond today's test to the probable fate of those who make the raid. The Wellington bomber duly arrives, the bomb is dropped, and is watched through binoculars by a dozen pairs of eyes (including ours, since we again see RAF film of the original tests, through a binocular frame that disguises its poorer quality compared to the 1955 footage). This time the bomb bounces exuberantly, with a loud musical chord accompanying each landing and watery 'splash' music in between. Gibson and Wallis hug each other, shout and gambol around like schoolboys after a goal has been scored, infectiously lowering the tension that has been so carefully created. That process is then completed by a final comic exchange in the car, as Wallis receives the enthusiastically insincere congratulations of his would-be executioners and cigars are handed round (our smarmy friend from the MAP appreciatively sniffing at his for the rest of the scene). Asked how wonderful it must be to conceive of such a remarkable idea all on his own and then see it succeed, Wallis mischievously admits that it was not actually his idea at all, but Lord Nelson's. How can this be? Apparently Nelson could increase the destructive power of cannonballs by getting them to ricochet off the water, 'but there's some evidence to suggest that during the battle of the Nile he dismissed the French flagship with a yorker'. This irreverent sending-up of the language of history and sport, usually treated so respectfully in British war films, is too much for the civil servants, who exchange pitying looks behind Wallis's back, and are clearly thinking that genius and eccentricity are indeed all too closely related. The Nelsonian touch was a comment made by Wallis at the time.

The mood remains light over the next four scenes, in which the training sequences of the film move towards the raid itself. First, the problem of releasing the bomb in the perfect place is solved by the RAF's 'backroom boys', with something that looks like 'a sixpenny coathanger' but which proves to work perfectly. This, like Gibson's idea for using spotlights to check altitude, is a classic presentation of the ingenuity of the British at war – a few bits of wood and two nails and, hey presto, a bomb-aiming device. In fact, it proved difficult to use, since the bomb-aimer actually needed to keep both hands free, and could not do this while using the new sight, so many of them adapted the idea with a variation of their own, painting marks on the Lancaster's perspex observation dome which would, when lined up with the Mohne's twin towers, indicate exact distance.

Specially adapted aircraft are also due to arrive, the only problem now being the difficulty of maintaining morale when the men don't know where they are going or when. In reality, Cochrane was by then warning Bomber Command that the raid must go ahead forthwith lest the men lose the edge of fitness and enthusiasm to which they were by now 'keyed'. In the film the problem is solved by a calculated decision to allow them to 'blow off steam' when they are next ragged as do-nothings by a rival squadron. We cut straight to the mess, where there is little to do but read magazines. Until, that is, the officers of 57 squadron enter, and one of them (an uncredited Gerald Harper) boasts of his 'sixteen ops in the last two months', and asks, 'What are you fellows going to do when you've worn out those armchairs?' Our heroes rise slowly to their feet ('Joke, you know. Can't you take it?'), and on Trevor-Roper's 'We're getting a little tired of it. Come on, chaps. Off with their bags', a tremendous scrimmage ensues as members of both squadrons try to remove each other's trousers. In his office, conscientiously studying maps, Gibson grins at the racket going on in the corridor (though the dog seems puzzled, a nice piece of editing) until summoned to meet Whitworth outside. He carefully locks away his map, then picks his way through a corridor in which trouserless bodies and scrums of men are everywhere. He pauses to rescue one of his men from the avenging 57 squadron and receives heartfelt thanks from Flight Lieutenant Maltby (George Baker): 'Thank you, sir. Saved my life. Never forget it.' There is grim irony here, for Maltby might well need life-saving in a few hours, though he will actually be one of the survivors. The scene as a whole is a telling reminder of just how much life these young men have, precisely before so many of them lose it – though pretty tame when compared to the binges that Gibson reported as inseparable from Bomber Command's domestic life. It is, on the other hand, just the sort of scene that led Richard Todd to conclude that they could capture 'the breezy, friendly atmosphere of an actual RAF squadron' only because so many actors remembered their own recent time in the services.[3]

Reaching the front of the building, straightening his tie and doing up buttons that have come adrift in the fracas, Gibson quickly reassures Whitworth that the noises of uproar are harmless. Whitworth's reaction suggests that such riots are not unusual on his station. And then, just when we are not prepared for it, Whitworth tells Gibson that weather conditions mean that the raid must take place tomorrow evening. (So tight has been the timing that the special bombs are only just arriving at Scampton – very close to the actual last-minute arrival of the bombs and the adapted Lancasters.) Gibson is instantly down to earth, and shows his relief: 'Good … Glad we're going.' He will now 'break up that show in there and get the boys to bed'. There follows an eloquent silence as neither knows how to end their conversation – Gibson may be going to his death and Whitworth will have to order the raid to go ahead. He can think of nothing to say, except – eventually – 'I'll see you in the morning. Goodnight, Guy' (with a very light touch on the shoulder). Though Whitworth has earlier said, 'We're old friends', neither he nor anyone else has called Gibson 'Guy', and nobody will again in the whole film (the real Whitworth apparently called Gibson 'Gibby', but this greater familiarity is being saved up by Sherriff for a single use later). Gibson's response is 'Goodnight', without his usual 'sir'. Use of the first name and dropping of rank is the nearest that these officers can get to a verbal expression of feeling, and when reviewers commented on the film's admirable restraint and its avoidance of stiff-upper-lip heroics it was just this type of moment that they had in mind. It rings absolutely true.

THE RAID

Almost exactly half of the film has now gone by; the rest will take place entirely within the twenty-four-hour period between the morning before the raid and the morning of the survivors' return to Scampton. (These events took two days in fact, but their telescoping into one morning–afternoon–evening–night–morning sequence gives continuous momentum.) The sequence therefore once again begins slowly, but with music now carrying more weight. Dawn breaks over Scampton to the accompaniment of a minor-key version of the march theme, played menacingly on muted brass, and we see Lancasters poetically silhouetted against the early morning sky. As the music modulates into the major key, now played softly on strings, the squadron assembles for its final briefing. If that hint of the big tune (not heard since the opening credits, an hour earlier) led us to expect a swift move into action, then we were misled, for it dies away as Gibson, Wallis and Whitworth stride purposefully into the briefing, and there is neither martial music nor action for another twelve minutes of tension-building. Those few critics who complained that the film's music was too much and too loud must surely have been reacting to the ubiquity of 'The Dam Busters' March' outside the film, on the radio and in the hit parade of 1955, rather than in the film itself, for it is doled out very sparingly indeed on the soundtrack.

Security requires that the doors are closed on the final briefing – but we do not need to hear it anyway, for we already know what the aircrews are now being told for the first time. We do, though, hear enough of the beginning and end of the meeting to see (often through reaction shots) how keen the men are to do the job that they have in front of them, how relaxed and informal is the question and answer session (but with Gibson effortlessly dealing with the questions – he's answered them in his own mind already), and with Wallis becoming increasingly emotional: 'Well, there it is, that's what the bomb does. The rest is for you ... And may I say good luck to you.' These excerpts from the briefing have been intercut with pictures of the technicians preparing, fuelling and arming planes out on the airfield. They are also intercut by the film's first tragedy: 'Nigger' is on the loose, but cannot join Gibson in his meeting and is sent away by an RAF policeman. He then lopes around the base,

7. *Gibson briefs his senior squadron officers. Mickey Martin (Bill Kerr) is
second from left, and second from right is Henry Maudslay (Richard
Thorp, latterly Alan Turner of* Emmerdale).

is greeted by NCOs and RAF policemen before running out of the
front gate and being run over by a passing motorist – who, in the film,
does not stop. Gibson is therefore confronted by his batman as he leaves
the briefing with the news that his beloved dog is lying dead in the
guardroom. Crosby is clearly responsible for letting 'Nigger' out (and
hence not keen to break the news to his officer), while Gibson's abrupt
'I see' is not exactly forgiving. But the job must come first, and he
strides off to get on with it. The real Gibson was much affected by the
bad news and had a stand-up row with a carpenter who refused to make
him a coffin for the dog (they had, after all, been working day and night
to get the planes ready).

By this stage, we have also seen and identified the pilots of the first
wave of nine Lancasters, those on whom the film will now concentrate,
we have watched as pilots are briefed over a large model of the dam
(helpfully reminding us of the dams' geography), and we have eaves-
dropped as their radio operators are briefed with the codewords to be
telegraphed back from the dam area: 'Goner' will signify a hit on a dam,

'Nigger' a breach in the Mohne dam, and 'Dinghy' a breach in the Eder. There appears to be no codeword for breaching the Sorpe dam, the film's RAF showing here considerable powers of foresight (as it was not breached, no such message was ever sent but codewords were of course prepared). We've also been retold, along with the aircrews, how important it all is: 'Tonight you're going to have the chance to hit the enemy harder and more destructively than any small force has done before.'

Now comes the immediate prelude to the raid, a slow sequence beginning with supper in the mess, enlivened only by the pay officer's feeble attempt to get a share of the bacon and eggs reserved for flyers; at Scampton in 1943, the issue of two eggs to each flyer told the WRAFs that a raid would be on tonight. The mood is quiet, sober and serious, with few words exchanged and those a parody of British understatement: 'Are you flying tonight, sir?' 'That's the general idea.' There is also black humour; when Mickey Martin receives a mess bill, he decides to delay paying it until tomorrow – after the raid. When Gibson is asked by Young if he can have Gibson's next egg if he does not come back, the response is, 'You can have mine, if I can have yours' (Brickhill says that this was 'the usual chestnut before an "op" and Gibson brushed it aside with a few amiably-insulting remarks'.) The only discordant note is sounded by Wallis fretting over last-minute preparations, for the oil in the bomb-release gear has been found to be the wrong type, and he puts everyone on edge with his nervousness. He refuses food and when Gibson obliges him to drink a cup of coffee, he stares straight through the offer of sugar. Nothing more clearly separates the younger men of action and the older man of ideas than Wallis's inability now to accept their collective fate.

Gibson patrols the airfield, making last-minute checks, and when he meets a groundstaff sergeant (Ewen Solon, a gem of a performance in a typical role; he would shortly be Sergeant Lucas in BBC television's classic *Maigret* series), he makes arrangements for 'Nigger' to be buried just outside Gibson's office, and at midnight, 'just about the time we're going in to the job over there' (Gibson actually asked for the burial at that time, but did *not* say why). He shakes off his dark mood, which can be shared only with the older, non-flying, NCO, and greets Hopgood (as he actually did in 1943) with, 'Hallo, Hoppy! Tonight's the night. Tomorrow we'll have a party.' The leader's task is to be encouraging and brave, whatever is going on inside, exactly as Gibson had argued in *Enemy Coast Ahead*. Back in the barracks, there's no apparent problem with the men's morale anyway, but the last-minute tasks of writing a letter, winding up a clock, reading, and otherwise putting affairs in order, all indicate what is going on in their minds. These scenes also point forward to the empty bedrooms that we shall see later. The squadron's archetypal Australians are still helpfully irrepressible. Since the laundry has returned, Leggo decides on a clean shirt and a fresh shave, since, 'If we have to bail out, you never know who we might meet'. 'There's no point in me bothering,' responds Martin. 'If we come down together and there happen to be two about, I'm bound to get the ugly one.'

In Gibson's office, the last-minute work is clearing files from the in-tray (putting the squadron's work in order, rather than his own), and while doing this he accidentally comes across 'Nigger's' leash. Intensely moved, he looks across at the scratch-marks that the dog has made on the door. For several seconds, there is a tug at the heart-strings harder than the film allows for any human bereavement. There's a swift inter-play of emotions on Richard Todd's face in close-up, pleasurable and amused memories of the dog in the past, pain at his loss, and then the need to keep a cap on his feelings for the good of the squadron. The leash is swiftly dropped into the wastebasket and the scene dissolves to an exterior shot of the airfield. In a lay-out reminiscent of newsreels and later feature films of the airfields of 1940, as fighter pilots awaited the order to go and meet their fate, 617 squadron lounges in a series of carefully composed groups: five men (surprisingly *not* the Australians this time) play an impromptu game of cricket, two friends share a quiet confidence, three men laugh over the smell of mess coffee in a flask. As the camera pans slowly across, Gibson's own crew come into frame last, with Sergeant Pulford playing chess with a fellow NCO, four officers playing pontoon (a nice 'People's War' joke this). All through the sequence, from the beginning in Gibson's office, we have again heard on the soundtrack the march tune, slow, muted and in a minor key, a static but threatening undertow.

Gibson, Wallis and Whitworth wander among the crews lounging on the grass, then there are inaudible final wishes of luck, hand-shakings, the stubbing out of Gibson's last cigarette, and his purposeful move towards his own crew, with the laconic, 'Well, chaps, my watch says it's time to go'. Gibson's men get up, immediately but not precipitately, and take station behind him, while other crews also gather and move off to their transport. The Gibson crew moves steadily towards us, the camera's low angle increasing both their stature and the deliberation of their

8. *Air Vice Marshal Cochran (Ernest Clark) offers good wishes to Gibson (Richard Todd) and his crew just before they take off for the raid. At left is Trevor-Roper (Brewster Mason), second from left is Pulford (Robert Shaw), and fifth from left is Spafford (Nigel Stock).*

movements. All the while, the music swells and thrusts towards the march tune, slowly modulating into the major key, and launches forth on full orchestra only as the wheels begin to move and a procession of vehicles carry the warriors to their steeds. The march lasts for only 45 seconds, but it is the first time in the film that the big tune has been played right through, and it carries a huge emotional punch.

Once at the aircraft, however, music quickly fades out, and the rest of the squadron's departure is accompanied only by the diegetic music of Rolls-Royce engines. The crews greet their planes, pilots signing as they take delivery from the groundstaff, some nervously patting their bombs, hugely pregnant beneath the Lancasters' bellies. There are last little nods between friends as crews climb aboard. Gibson's own entry is interrupted by Cochrane's arrival to pay his respects. This occasions brief compliments on both sides, then Cochrane briskly wishes Gibson, 'Good luck', repeating it more casually to his crew – the command and the mission having a higher priority than the men. Something of the

1943, REALITY : Gibson (on steps) and his crew before the take-off

1954, RE-CREATION : Trevor-Roper (played by Brewster Mason), Pulford (Robert Shaw), Deering (Peter Assinder), Spafford (Nigel Stock), Hutchinson (Anthony Doonan), Gibson (Richard Todd), Taerum (Brian Nissen)

9. *The real Gibson and his crew prepare to take off in 1943. Note the remarkable resemblances of the 1954 actors to the 1943 originals.*

artificiality of a visit from the top brass is nicely captured here. When Cochrane inspected the squadron in early May, air navigator Charlie Williams wrote home to his family in Bannockburn, Queensland, that 'it caused all the section commanders a good deal of worry, and they were glad to see him go'.[4]

The interruption does, however, provide for another departure line, Gibson's matter-of-fact 'Come on, then'. It also provides, when Cochrane's car is first heard arriving, a nicely framed moment of stasis, with Todd paused at the top of the ladder as he leads the way into his Lancaster, the other six crew members below him, grouped with five to the left and one to the right, all looking past the camera towards Cochrane's apparent arrival. This is an exact re-creation of a still photograph taken on 16 May 1943, as Gibson's actual crew were captured by an RAF publicity photographer, and was a photograph much used in the British press on the following day, later reprinted in Gibson's autobiography. This is, therefore, at that crucial moment of the bombers' take-off, visible evidence both of Michael Anderson's painstaking research and pre-planning, and of the overriding documentary desire to show as well as to tell the story right. There were many such filmed re-creations of 1943 photographs.

The last crews board their aircraft, pilots take their places, a signal flare is fired, engines roar into life, chocks are removed, and each aircraft edges forwards. So extensive had been Richard Todd's training by an RAF instructor in the cockpit of his Lancaster that he felt he could almost have flown one himself by the time that location filming was over, and he was indeed allowed to drive (on the ground) as his Lancaster taxied towards the runway for take-off. Finally, we see the pilot's hands on the controls, the throttle is inched forwards and three flights, each of three Lancasters, take off in the gathering darkness (it once again having got dark surprisingly quickly). The film's aerial photography was generally praised in 1955, as indeed it deserved to be; these take-off sequences are no doubt one reason why some reviewers considered the Lancasters to be the film's real stars. A particularly effective moment comes as the second flight fly over Lincoln, the cathedral momentarily standing out against the night sky and the river glinting beyond. Coincidentally, it was identifying Lincoln looking just like that that allowed the real Gibson to find his way back to Scampton on his first night flight in 1939.

As the engine roar dies away, Wallis and Whitworth are left back on the ground, and thus begins a relentless alternation of longish scenes in the aircraft with brief moments back in Lincolnshire; this will last for half an hour, a device taken straight from Brickhill's book. Sensing Whitworth's presence behind him, Wallis remarks superfluously, 'I suppose there's not much *we* can do – *except wait*', his final two slow words the harbinger of his terrible night to come. Cochrane has waited to take them back to Grantham where Group has its operations room, and back they go.

We now see an extensive sequence in which the squadron flies over the North Sea, crosses the Dutch coast and navigates its way to the Ruhr. At first the mood is light-hearted, with 'conversations' flashed by lamp from plane to plane and Gibson confirming that they will indeed get 'screechers' on the following night – 'biggest binge of all time!' These men are in good heart. Then they cross the Dutch coast (bomb-aimers of the second and third flights each announcing, 'Enemy coast ahead', the title of the Gibson's book). The mood becomes more tense, and pilots button their radio-masks in place so as to be in permanent radio contact. Nothing much happens to the planes on which we are concentrating, but the risk is clearly there, for Grantham receives the news that the squadron's northern wave, heading for the Sorpe dam, 'ran into trouble on the coast. McCarthy's going on to the Sorpe on his own.' For those who had concentrated during the earlier briefing, this carries the message that four aircraft may already be lost (though, in fact, while two had gone down, technical problems forced another two to return home without ever reaching Germany). We hear no more about the Sorpe dam during the film, a misleading emphasis since the failure to breach it materially limited the effect of the other successes. Back at Grantham this news, coming after waiting that is already hard to endure, is deeply felt. Bomber Harris, who earlier arrived at Grantham with a brisk, 'Hello, Cocky! Cheer up, Wallis. This is your night as well as theirs', now swallows hard at the news of twenty-eight men probably lost, tilting down his head so that the peak of his cap covers his eyes.

Even with the first wave of bombers there has been plenty of evidence of the dangers involved. A side-shot of Gibson in the cockpit allows us to see (by back-projection) the Dutch countryside flashing past from an altitude that seems not much different from the view from a train. There is also, when flying along a canal, a moment in which the low-flying planes almost crash into pylons, but timely forewarning by Gibson's navigator allows the pilots to climb steeply over them before resuming the low-level course. This quick threat is passed without comment, unlike a similar panic-climb in training which had produced the Antipodean yelp, 'This is bladdy dyngerous!' Nobody would say

10. *The attacking Lancasters run into anti-aircraft searchlights and flak.*

such a thing when on the job, though the audience certainly thinks it. If we assume that men at war would really have been swearing the night away (as has been alleged by critics of the polite language in Humphrey Jennings' *Fires were Started*), then we are probably wrong. When one of the northern wave of Lancasters dipped into the sea – losing its bomb, filling the aircraft with water and then almost drowning the rear gunner in his turret when the plane climbed steeply to regain height – all that was heard over the intercom was a plaintive, 'Christ, it's wet at the back. You've lost the mine.' Understatement may well have been getting it 'right'.

Confirmation of the danger comes quite soon, though, when the third trio of bombers runs into flak – and by now German gunners would be good and ready. From a camera-plane's perspective, and in reaction shots on Z for Zebra, we see B for Bertie hit by anti-aircraft fire, burst into flames and crash in a fireball. No words are spoken and the other two Lancasters fly on, gradually getting out of range. Up ahead, Gibson in G for George encounters a bank of searchlights and ack-ack guns that had *not* been foreseen, radioing back to warn the others, and we see his whole crew in action, pilot flying on as nearby explosions shake the plane, gunners firing furiously at the lights, navigator plotting on as if no battle was raging around him. This time, there are no casualties. There is, however, no hint here of pilots getting lost (it was extremely difficult to navigate at such a low level and the later waves had the additional problem that Gibson's first team had created a lake in the Ruhr valley that was not on their maps), or of individual planes losing each other in the dark and not finding their formation again. At the time, as a survivor later remembered, it was 'all very much fit and make fit, despite what has been said afterwards'.

Our third visit to the Grantham control room produces not only information about heavy casualties in the northern wave but also news that 'Gibson's formation should be nearly at the Mohne'. The film thus moves to its climax, and tension is raised both by an increased urgency in the delivery of lines and by more rapid cutting. Much is done to manipulate viewers' reactions through the arts of the cutting room, as here, where shorter intervals between camera shots create the impression that the pace of events has speeded up. In the long daytime sequence at Scampton, the average shot lasts for 10.5 seconds; for the flight out, this is already down to 8.7 seconds, and for the attack itself, it falls to just 6.1 seconds between each cut.

Crews of the leading bombers now see for the first time their prime target, the Mohne dam, as they try to reconnoitre while dodging its protective flak: 'My goodness, it's big, isn't it? Can we really break that?' There are still eight bombers of the nine that set out in Gibson's leading formation, each answering the radio call with, 'Here, Leader', and Gibson orders the attack one at a time, he himself going first. He also orders, in the same matter-of-fact tone, that M for Mother should take command 'if anything happens' (as orders had laid down) and tells his own crew to 'stand by to pull me out of the seat if I get hit'. G for George's attack goes smoothly ('This is fine. I can see everything', chortles Spafford in the bomb-aimer's bay), and he scores a direct hit ('Nice work, skipper ... Bang-on, skipper'). There is a large explosion and a wall of water shoots skywards. There's a triumphant cry from the flight engineer of, 'It's gone, We've done it!', but Trevor-Roper chips in deflatingly with, 'We haven't. It's still there.' It was clear, however, from Wallis's later investigations that Gibson's bomb had been dropped short and exploded away from the dam wall (though not in the film where Gibson the leader *has* to score a hit).

Back at Grantham, the tension is already unbearable, and the fact

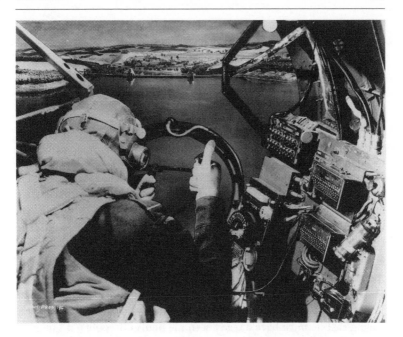

11. *Gibson's Lancaster goes in to attack the Mohne dam, with 'Spam'*
Spafford (Nigel Stock) about to drop the first bouncing-bomb.

that we already know that they are in for a disappointment adds to
this feeling. The signals officer receives a Morse message, hopefully
announces 'Goner', then, after a pause, a flat 'That's all'. It's a palpable
hit, but no breach. Wallis ruefully remarks, 'I hoped one bomb might do
it' (which, when the film's imaginary hits are discounted, it probably
did). The others present, all RAF senior officers, apparently already
wondering how to cope with the eccentric's crushing disappointment,
uneasily move away from him with embarrassed glances. With Gibson
and his boys in the air, Wallis is the only one back home who seems to
believe it is possible to succeed.

At the Mohne dam, it is now the turn of M for Mother, but Hopgood
mistimes his approach, and drops the bomb too late. It bounces right
over the dam (as Wallis had warned in an earlier scene), and his Lancaster
is caught by the bomb's impact and itself explodes. Gibson and Pulford
meet each other's eyes and quickly look away. When Martin's P for
Popsie (a signal code almost as politically incorrect as 'Nigger' – even
in 1943 it was supposed to be 'P for Peter') goes in for his turn, Gibson
flies in alongside to act as decoy for the anti-aircraft fire. This is (his-

torically accurate) heroism of a high order, and passes entirely without comment. It is after all one thing to 'press home the attack' in an aircraft that has a powerful bomb to drop, something quite different to fly in at low level simply to get shot at. In the event it is P for Popsie which is hit – the only time we experience a hit from inside the bomber. The flight engineer shouts 'Starboard wing's hit', and the plane shudders, but Martin responds with 'Starboard outer [tank]'s empty, thank God!' and calmly reports that he's still in control.

This is now the second direct hit on the dam (actually the real Mickey Martin also missed, his bomb sheering off and exploding against the shoreline), but we do not see the result of it, so we have to share the uncertainty in Grantham as the signal comes through. Once again it's 'Goner', and an agonizing pause before another flat, 'That's all'. The RAF men leave Wallis entirely alone. It's now A for Apple's turn to attack and there are two decoys to draw the flak. Another hit, another spout of upward-leaping water, another agonizing wait in Grantham, this time before any message at all. (When Richard Todd later tells Michael Redgrave, 'You've had a worse night than any of us', you can't help feeling that he must have already seen the film.) Of course, it's another 'Goner ... That's all'. The senior officers are now quite obviously thinking that they were crazy ever to entertain such an idea as a bouncing-bomb, and though Whitworth moves to comfort Wallis, he finds that he can think of nothing to say, and leaves him in his dumb agony.

J for Johnny (Maltby) now produces the fourth hit, and the fourth waterspout, and Gibson grimly tells Dave Shannon to stand by for his turn at what increasingly seems like a pointless exercise. But then, with no warning, the wall of the dam begins first to leak, then to disintegrate, and finally topples forwards as water crashes through a widening breach. This is perhaps the film's best special effect, just as the waterspouts after each explosion (obviously sea water, much magnified) had been the weakest.

No one bomb had done the trick, but the four 'hits' have allowed the weight of water pressure to force its way through, an unhistorical tribute to team effort. We hear, 'It's gone! My God!', while a voice on the radio adds, 'You've done it, skipper. Well done', so concentrating attention back on the leader. Gibson himself tells Shannon to cancel his attack, sends the damaged and empty Lancasters home, and leads the rest off to the Eder. In Grantham, the tension is thick enough to cut with a knife; when the signals officer takes the call, his face is seconds ahead of his voice in revealing the news, 'It's Nigger! It's gone!', and there are

12. *The control room in Grantham, with Bomber Harris (Basil Sydney)*
and Group Captain Whitworth (Derek Farr) trying to console Wallis
(Michael Redgrave) when the first bombs do not destroy the dams.

congratulations from everyone for Wallis, now dumb with pleasure,
flapping his arms about like a drunken penguin. In view of the fictitious
over-centrality of Wallis's role to the film's scientific plot, Harris's
'You've done it, Wallis!' has a crucial, confirming importance.

Whereas the breaching of the Mohne dam took eleven minutes of
film, the subsequent attack on the Eder gets only five, so avoiding either
repetition or anti-climax. It does, however, set different problems, for
although there is no anti-aircraft flak, the geographical location is much
more difficult ('Take your time, and mind the mountain on the other
side ... ') In any case, there are only three bombs left and it took four
to breach the Mohne. Shannon makes his attack but mistimes the approach, pulls up steeply and saves his plane but has not managed to
drop his bomb. The wise Gibson tells him to wait a bit rather than try
again straightaway, so giving his crew time to settle down. (The real
Shannon had to make several abortive efforts before dropping his bomb,
but to show this would undermine the squadron's apparent skill.) Z for
Zebra follows, also mistimes his flight, drops the bomb too late and

crashes into the hill opposite. Once again we read a death in Gibson's eyes, all that he can act with above the flying mask. L for Leather (a nice pun) scores a hit, with no visible effect, and the senior men in Grantham are again so fraught that they unceremoniously wave away a WRAF with mugs of cocoa without so much as a 'No, thank you'. The juniors, with less responsibility for what is going on, take what's on offer (it is now, after all, about 3 a.m., and they will be up all night).

N for Nuts is now attacking, warned by Gibson that, 'You've got the last bomb, Les, so take your time', a reminder of responsibility not especially welcomed, to judge from the exchange of glances in the cockpit. It's very tight to fly low through the valley and get over the hills opposite, but there is a direct hit, and though the camera and soundtrack illustrate the subsequent hair-raising climbing and banking of the Lancaster from inside the cockpit, we hear an explosion. This time, the dam bursts quickly, collapsing from the top, with water again surging through the breach. There is no radio-talk after that second success, since we cut straight back to Grantham with the normally flat voice of the signals officer exploding into, 'It's Dinghy! They've done it! They've got the Eder dam as well.' ('Dinghy' Young himself, though, is already dead.) Wallis's mute pleasure is now less restrained, giving nods of acceptance to the congratulations that rain down from both sides, but he cannot actually speak. Harris tells him, 'Wallis, when you first came to me with this, I didn't believe a word you said. Now you can sell me a pink elephant.' (Harris actually said this to Wallis when the Mohne was breached, but the film has saved it as a second tribute from Bomber Command's father-figure at the film's climax.)

Martial music has underscored the dialogue since the moment at which the second dam burst, and it continues through the next sequence, with Gibson telling everyone to 'Scram for home' while the screen begins to show us the devastation that his bombers have wrought. At first there are simply shots of swirling water and powerful waves surging around, then we see the flooding of a train in motion and of factories. Finally, we see flooded towns, fields, factories and marshalling yards. These last were filmed in 1954 from a camera-plane in the Ruhr valley itself, when it was fortuitously flooded while *The Dam Busters* was being filmed. We there-fore see lots of damage, certainly on a scale to match expectations raised earlier in the film, but we see no drownings – the only people visible in the flood scenes being the workers who escape rising waters by climbing their factories' stairs. The actual bombers watched fascinated as distant headlights showed cars racing away from the flood, their lights first going green and then going out altogether as cars and passengers were simultaneously submerged; dramatic stuff described by Brickhill, but not in the film. Without any comment or analysis, the film therefore allows us to see a 'clean' hit at a strategic target crucial to Germany's war effort, and does its bit to bolster memories of the legitimate work of Bomber Command. All of this has been accompanied by music that was at times dark, sometimes swirling around with the swirling water. Eventually there is a triumphant reprise of 'The Dam Busters' March', but from this time on the film winds down into a reflective coda. In this quiet closure, the average length of each camera shot is a very slow 19 seconds.

THE RETURN

As flooded Germany dissolves into an English grassy field, with a distant bomber coming in to land, the music drops down to strings playing the big tune, but quietly and more elegaically than in triumph. Over the next couple of minutes we see the return of P for Popsie, which taxies right over the camera, its wing visibly damaged, its men emerging weary with exhaustion. We see the crews of later arrivals gratefully receiving warm drinks and gripping each other encouragingly on the shoulder as they move to the debriefing tables, and we see the Australian pair return to their room, so shattered that they lie mutely down to sleep, still booted and fully clothed. Throughout this two minutes, music plays quietly but no words are spoken, one of those sequences that – though it is all carefully thought out and acted – seems to belong to a documentary rather than a feature film.

Film of Gibson's own return with his crew (he actually began his debrief with the words 'It was a wizard party, sir … '), their leaving the plane, his striding over to the headquarters building with Whitworth and Cochrane, the chalking-up of the word 'MISSING' on several lines of a name-board that already contains the word too often, are all shown to the accompaniment of a BBC newsreader announcing the raid's success to the British public. The style of the broadcast, the authority of the BBC, and the instantly recognizable voice of wartime newsreader Frank Phillips, would have collectively endowed that announcement with great credibility at the time of the film's release. It is the only part of the concluding section that tells us what to think about what we have seen during the film, and needs to be quoted in full:

This is London. The Air Ministry has just issued the following com-

13. *The weary returning crews are debriefed at Scampton, David Maltby (George Baker) sitting at centre left.*

muniqué. In the early hours of this morning, a force of Lancasters of Bomber Command led by Wing Commander Guy Gibson, DSO, DFC, attacked with mines the dams of the Mohne and Sorpe reservoirs. These control over two-thirds of the water storage of the Ruhr basin. Reconnaissance later established that the Mohne dam had been breached over a length of one hundred yards, and that the power station below had been swept away by the resulting floods. The Eder dam, which controls the headwaters of the Weser and Fulde valleys and operates several power stations, was also attacked and reported as breached. Photographs show the river below the dam in full flood. The attacks were pressed home from a very low level, with great determination and coolness, in the face of fierce resistance. Eight of the Lancasters are missing.

This was the actual BBC broadcast of 18 May 1943, but since it here becomes the film's verdict on the raid, its inclusion suggests that nothing learned since 1943 has added anything of significance to what was believed at the time – which was far from the case, as Wallis knew well from his investigations at the Mohne dam. To be pedantic, we might also notice the impossibility of the BBC broadcasting at 6 a.m. an account which depended on reconnaissance of the Ruhr in daylight following a raid that took place after midnight, but perhaps the film-makers have by this stage earned the suspension of our disbelief.

Accuracy of detail would in any case matter much more if the film ended on the stirring note of the BBC broadcast, but it does not. The last four minutes are used by Sherriff and Anderson to bring us gently back to an earth where war is to be regretted rather than celebrated. The screenplay and direction do not *say* any such thing, but they show us with documentary clarity scenes that draw us to that conclusion. First come a couple of minutes with neither dialogue nor music, in which the airfield mourns its dead. As the BBC broadcast, with its reference to eight missing crews, dies away, we see breakfast in the mess, unshaven men gratefully receiving their 'next egg' but eating silently and subdued, many of the tables empty. Then the camera wanders through empty barrack-rooms, focusing on Dinghy Young's disconsolate batman and on the oar on the wall that celebrates his rowing blue, on another man's letter home now to be dispatched to the next of kin, and on the clock, so carefully wound up before the raid but whose owner will never return to read the time. It is still only five past six in the morning.

Finally, the film cuts to an airfield roadway along which Gibson is striding, stopped in his tracks by the ungainly running figure of Wallis, who asks, 'Is it true? All those fellows lost?' Yes, Gibson confirms, eight planes missing, four in known circumstances, four simply not answering radio calls since midnight. He adds the professional's opinion that 'The flak was bad, worse than I expected'. Wallis is, however, thinking on a different level, and so are the audience: '*Fifty-six men.* If I'd known it was going to be like this, I'd never have started it.' If we do think this, then our sympathies are not where the film wants them to be, for Gibson offers, without theatricality, the absolution that Wallis needs. 'You mustn't think that way. If all those fellows had known from the beginning that they wouldn't be coming back, they'd have gone for it just the same. There isn't a single one that would have dropped out. I knew them all and I know that's true.' There follows kindly meant advice to Wallis to get some rest after his terrible night, and the suggestion that the base doctor could arrange the appropriate sleeping pill. This is a moment of personal closeness, with Wallis responding to 'Gibby' (an affectionate word used months earlier in Brickhill's book, but saved by Sherriff for the last page of the script, though he never allows Todd to call Redgrave 'Wally', as Gibson actually did) that he should 'turn in' too. But this he

14. *The final scene: Wallis (Michael Redgrave) with Gibson (Richard Todd) in the authentic German 'Mae West' jacket, as worn by the real Gibson.*

cannot do, for 'I have to write some letters first', a reply that drains the returning life from Wallis's face and ends their brief conversation. It is impossible for either to add even a word of farewell, much less one of consolation. Wallis and Gibson are everyone else's heroes this morning but they know too much of the downside of success to risk congratulating one another. Instead, Gibson turns smartly away towards his office to start the commanding officer's most dreaded task, Wallis stumbles out of shot, and as the march tune surges up for one last time, Gibson walks on without deviation down his lonely road, while a saluting sergeant and the crossing of a distant lorry hint that in the wartime RAF life goes on.

The film's final credits are played out over the completion of the big tune, and, though they do not include everyone who has uttered lines in the film, they do strive for every detail in describing the officers, each of whom gets his full title and decorations and, in the case of post-war regulars, their subsequent rank too. Hence, Bill Kerr ('Mickey' in most of the dialogue) has played 'Flight Lieutenant H. B. Martin, DSO, DFC, AFO (now Wing Commander)' while poor old Crosby loses his name altogether and is listed (thirty-eighth out of thirty-eight) simply as 'Wing

Commander Gibson's batman'. Nor does Harold Goodwin playing Crosby seem to have tried to make him much like the actual Crosby described in *Enemy Coast Ahead* – an elderly, lugubrious northerner – which suggests that rather less research had gone into this role than into the officers and gentlemen higher up the credits. The film ends, then, as it began, claiming authenticity but foregrounding the officers (even the Australian proletarians) at the expense of the other ranks.

Since few would have stayed in the cinema to read the credits, and hence risk also having to stand through the national anthem, memories of the film for its initial audience would have rested on the last ten minutes. The anonymous reviewer in *Time and Tide*, giving much credit to Sherriff's script, which 'keeps mainly out of sight, and, when it does come into the open, registers the more heavily', concluded with a re-lieved catalogue of how the film *might* have ended in cruder hands. 'The deeply moving ending is achieved by cleverly oblique implication. The story itself was good enough and they have let it be. No sobbing WAAFs calling B for Baker, no merciless injections of Other Rank badinage, no misty-eyed barmaids at the station pub, no brave upward glances at throbbing skies ... Which is just as it should be.' (This catalogue smartly dismisses the final shots of *Mrs Miniver* and *The Way to the Stars*, among others.) Nor was it easy to get that last scene between Todd and Redgrave right, even though the screenwriter had given them (as Laurence Thompson put it) a scene 'as fine as anything Sherriff has written since *Journey's End*'. They had to film it almost at the very start of the location schedule, with little chance earlier to act their characters. But (as Redgrave told Thompson), while most filming was witnessed by a crowd of RAF men and their families, they were now kept right out of the way so as not to distract the actors. Redgrave remembered that 'Todd and I didn't talk to each other or anybody else while we were waiting, just walked up and down. I was saying to myself – no, no, that makes it sound a very deliberate process, which it isn't – but it was something like saying to myself, "You've been up all night, listening to all this. Fifty-six people missing. I must see Gibson. I must see Gibson."' That inner fixation, a touch of the Stanislavskian 'Method', which Red-grave disdained for Shakespeare but was happy to use in films, produced the ungainly lope with which he flops into shot and the scene never then loses the tension built up before the camera began to roll. It is as fine a moment as actor, screenwriter or director ever managed in a film, and coming at the very end, its effect is devastating.[5]

FOUR
Post-Production

Almost a year elapsed between the completion of filming and the première, and a further three months more before general release on 5 September 1955, an interval that facilitated a good technical job in post-production and the preparation of a big promotional campaign. The extensive forward planning involved in such long lead times had guaranteed the availability of experienced men in other key roles, notably Erwin Hillier as director of photography and Richard Best as editor. This was an unusually difficult technical job: Laurence Thompson noted that in order to get a single shot of Gibson looking out of his cockpit to view the dam, while flak shoots past in the night sky and an another bomber passes below, it was necessary to shoot six separate 'travelling matts': a studio shot of Todd in the studio cockpit, the model dam, photographed flak, the countryside background to the model, an explosion (different model), and a Lancaster flying. Each had to be shot at exactly the right angle of vision, and each had to be in proportion to its size as viewed from that distance. To get that one shot, 300 preparatory drawings had been done by the art department. Best, like Anderson, had come up the hard way through the studios, learning on the job by working with such directors as Roy Boulting, David Lean and Herbert Wilcox. He was also a veteran of the Army Film Unit, where he had worked on such classic documentaries as *Desert Victory*, and his editing work no doubt helped to create the documentary feel that Anderson was seeking. He also seems to have shared in the conservative and patriotic values of the rest of the production team, enjoying most of all his work on war films *Ice Cold in Alex* and *The Dam Busters*, and later getting himself dropped by Tony Richardson from *Look Back in Anger* after unwisely saying that he did not like the play's 'anti-British' tone.[1]

So unusually long did this second interval seem for a film generally expected to be released before the end of 1954, and so keenly awaited, that the press began to speculate whether something had gone wrong. Possibly something had indeed delayed completion, for the *Daily Mail* (under the embarrassing headline 'Dam Bust Film Held Up by VC's Widow') reported that Associated British was locked in a copyright dispute with Gibson's widow. Eve Gibson (now Mrs Hyman) was apparently claiming that she had never given permission for the use of material in the film drawn from her late husband's book. Having heard about the film from a press clipping (she was now living in South Africa), she had written to demand a copy of the script, had immediately recognized sections drawn from *Enemy Coast Ahead* and set off forthwith for London: 'I am not concerned with the financial aspect – I am just very deeply hurt that they did not consult me. After all, I am the next-of-kin. I was the woman who received the pension.' She went on to reiterate the fact that this was nothing to do with money ('It simply is not true. I don't need it') or the desire for publicity ('I hate publicity').[2] In view of the exhaustive research among survivors and the next of kin undertaken by Brickhill, by Sherriff and by the production team and cast over four years, this seems an unlikely version of events. Eve Gibson *must* have known about the film being made, and there was certainly an air of the lady protesting too much in her denial of financial motivation. Richard Todd states categorically that he talked to her before acting the part of Guy Gibson, and she could hardly have failed to understand his reason for doing so. On the other hand, she had been far from close to Gibson in April–May 1943. Apart from the deterioration of their marriage, Bomber Command had laid down a ruling that no aircrew wives were to live within forty miles of their husbands' base, a rule that Gibson ruthlessly enforced at Scampton (which no doubt also facilitated his serial affairs with the WRAFs). Eve Gibson would therefore not have had much to tell anyone about what happened to her husband in the six weeks of his life covered by the film, but may have felt slighted not to have been more involved in the process of memorializing him.

Speaking for Associated British, Robert Clark's initial reaction was conciliatory, stating grandiloquently that ABPC would 'certainly pay compensation' if the widow's rights had been infringed: 'We are prepared to shoot the whole film again if necessary.' He was careful, though, to point out that the film was based on Brickhill's book – for which ABPC had already paid – and that if Brickhill had incorporated without permission material from Gibson, then this was really a matter for Brickhill and Gibson's widow, not for ABPC. Brickhill, meanwhile, had flown to New York to negotiate with Mrs Hyman's agents. There may be something more than coincidental in the fact that Gibson's father, who had seen the film (presumably only the rushes by that stage) on 15 July 1954, waited until October to write a letter to Robert Clark that was *extremely* helpful to the company. In that letter, he clearly stated that he had seen a script as early as 1952, had been corresponding with Brickhill and the company about a film for over three years, and was now quite happy with the film that they had made. It seems likely that the lining-up of Gibson's father with a ringing endorsement was arranged in anticipation of the attack from South Africa. Alexander Gibson's letter was printed in facsimile in the main publicity handout for *The Dam Busters*, so important was overt family approval deemed to be. The invisible irony was that Alexander Gibson was even more distant from Guy in spring 1943 than was Eve, having played little part at all in his life since leaving his marriage to Guy's mother years before. The whole spat may indeed have been mainly a family one between the father and the widow over the 'ownership' of Guy Gibson ten years after his death. Alexander Gibson's assurance that ABPC had got his hero-son right was not, therefore, worth very much as historical evidence, but as a property in the hands of ABPC's public relations men his letter was invaluable.

It is impossible to clarify half a century after the event the nature of the negotiations that followed, or the deal that was eventually struck, but when released in 1955, both opening titles and final release script admitted that it had been based on *both* Brickhill's book and Gibson's. It seems unlikely that such a credit would have been conceded without some accompanying financial concession to the copyright owner of the Gibson book. Whatever the deal, it did allow the film to be released without further embarrassment, for both Alexander Gibson and Eve Hyman attended the film's premières and were widely reported to have done so. ABPC had neutralized its problem and received unequivocal family endorsement.

THE SOUNDTRACK

One post-production process that contributed hugely to the film was the soundtrack, both in sound effects (roaring Rolls-Royce Merlin engines accompanying most of the flying scenes), and in music. Michael Anderson, who was able to play an active part in the post-production processes because his next assignment was in the same studio, remembers exceptional care going into every aspect of dubbing and sound mixing. 'Every schoolboy knows' (as Anthony Trollope would have put it) that

Eric Coates wrote the 'The Dam Busters', but neither schoolboys nor many adults know that he did not write the march for the film nor did he work on its production. Coates was an unlikely choice. He had written theme music, 'By a Sleepy Lagoon' for example, used for half a century for *Desert Island Discs*, and the 'Knightsbridge March' for BBC Radio's *In Town Tonight*, where the first use of the music provoked 20,000 letters to the BBC asking what the tune was, but these were ready-made pieces of music bought by the BBC off the peg, not commissioned pieces. And although in that generation there was a considerable cross-over between classical composers and film production, with Walton, Vaughan Williams and Bax all producing important film scores, Coates had never done so. He was reluctant to spend time writing music that would never be used, or be chopped around to suit the director's editing requirements. Presumably his tuneful world of 'light music' was already enough of a paying proposition anyway. He was, however, a very patriotic man. He had written music in honour of the royal family, war munitions workers, war savings and the capital city, and was keen to accept this job. Coates had written in 1943 (but never published or had much performed) a patriotic march in honour of the Eighth Army's victory at the Battle of Alamein. This he now reworked into 'The Dam Busters' March', so writing what was to become his most famous piece, though not a source of income before his early death in 1957, for he donated all the royalties to the RAF Benevolent Fund. The march has remained an exceptionally popular piece of music, included from time to time in Proms Concerts and still available at the end of the century in fourteen different recordings. In his autobiography, published in 1953 when he would have been starting work on the famous march, he wrote modestly that he was 'a very ordinary man'. His *Times* obituarist quoted this self-description and added patronizingly 'and so he was'. Though arguing that his music 'never rose above the unadventurous and the obvious', the obituary also explained that his works' 'enormous currency' was because 'he knew from his own nature what the ordinary man feels and thinks ... If his music is superficial, it is also sincere.' When due allowance is made for sneering by the musical establishment at a man who simply wrote good tunes – Coates fell between two highly respectable stools, classical music and 'really popular jazz', the perennial fate of the composer of 'light music' – there was no doubt a grain of truth in the explanation. Ordinary people do, after all, like good tunes such as the march from *The Dam Busters* (though that *Times* obituarist could not bring himself even to name it, smash hit that it was).[3] Alas, Coates could never repeat the trick, and his only later film score, the march *High Flight*, never caught on in the same way.

'The Dam Busters' March' is so instantly recognizable in modern Britain that it may not be obvious how much it is a derivative piece, its appeal lying partly in the very familiarity of its form, pace and scoring. The most obvious influences are the marches written by William Walton for the wartime films *Went the Day Well?* and *The First of the Few* (the latter's 'Spitfire Prelude' appropriately close in feel to Coates's march). What is less noticeable is the extent to which Walton's film marches are themselves derived from a classical tradition of period pieces for state occasions, especially coronations. Walton's own 'Crown Imperial' (1937) springs to mind, as does his 'Orb and Sceptre' (1953), written while *The Dam Busters* was already in the pre-production stage. Both are modelled on the 'Pomp and Circumstance' marches of Edward Elgar, written in part for an earlier coronation. All of these composers from Elgar to Coates owed such popular successes to the British tradition of military band music, which makes its impact largely through constant repetition on bandstands, parades and promenades (and latterly also on Classic FM). Coates's march is an archetype of such a classical march. After a fanfare-like, fugato opening, it begins as a sprightly quick-march which, after a short bridge passage, moves into a slower but uplifting trio section, the 'big tune'; the quick-march returns but this time the transitional section is longer, delaying a reprise of the big tune in the dominant key (pitched half an octave higher than when first played, and so even more upward-reaching, more exhilarating for community singing), before coming to a strong, upbeat cadence on solid chords. We need to remind ourselves, though, that Anderson had almost completed his work as director before first hearing Coates play through his march in a piano reduction, and it was only in the post-production phase that he was able to take account of its sonorous mood as it was sparingly dubbed on to the soundtrack.

By the time of its publication in sheet-music form in 1955 (the poster from the film on the cover), 'The Dam Busters' March' had acquired words with a patriotic appeal, just as 'Land of Hope and Glory' was matched to the *'nobilmente'* section of Elgar's greatest march. Though Carlene Mair wrote the words, they proved at least acceptable to Coates, and tell us something of his own attitude to the music of the film:

> Proudly, with high endeavour,
> We, who are young forever,

> Won the freedom of the skies,
> We shall never die!
> We who have made our story,
> Part of our Empire's glory,
> Know our names will still live on,
> While Britons fly![4]

Note the use of 'Empire', so closely related to the white dominions' presence in both 617 squadron in 1943 and the film of 1955 (though later editions feebly substituted 'country' for 'Empire'). Note, too, the unashamed homage that it offers, the reassurance of immortality that is essential to any effective war memorial, and the upbeat assumptions about Britain's future prospects. The song lyrics thus managed to match even such reviews of the film as that in the *News of the World*, headlined 'See It and be Proud'.[5]

Although the RAF's 'March Past' was its official anthem, this soon became secondary to 'The Dam Busters' March', which was first released on record by both the RAF Central Band and by the Sidney Torch Orchestra to coincide with release of the film. In those pre-rock days, this patriotic band music went straight into the bestsellers' list where it was rapidly joined by a third version recorded by BBC television's Billy Cotton Band, a version given extra authenticity by the superimposition of extracts from the film soundtrack ('OK, Leader, I'm going in now … '), just prior to the final return of the big theme. It has remained a patriotic favourite ever since. When CND was briefly resurgent during the final phase of the Cold War, the Ministry of Defence took to playing 'The Dam Busters' March', hugely amplified, to drown out the discordant sound of chanting around its airbases. In the 1990s it was still being tauntingly sung by English fans – with appropriate arm movements to suggest low flying – when German football teams visited grounds like Wembley or Everton's Goodison Park, to the utter incomprehension of the visiting supporters, it must be said. And when that bastion of the patriotic establishment, Sir Adrian Boult, always one of the first to sign the Tory candidate's nomination papers in his native Hampstead, celebrated his eightieth birthday in 1969, he served up a surprise to the assembled music-lovers in the Royal Festival Hall. After a concert consisting predictably of Elgar's Violin Concerto, Parry's 'Blest Pair of Sirens' and Vaughan Williams's 'London' symphony, Sir Adrian played as an encore 'The Dam Busters' March'. Live recordings indicate audible amazement changing to great pleasure and massive cheering as the LPO blazingly completed that big tune.

One or two reviewers argued that there was an excess of loud music in the film, just as a few were upset by 'ugly' engine noise, but very few even commented on the soundtrack, so relatively restrained is the use of the famous march. Here, the credit goes not to Coates but to Anderson, who decided when to use and when not to use music, but also to Leighton Lucas who took Coates's march and turned it into a film score. The quick-march section he discarded altogether, and the bridge passage is used only in the credits or to launch the march. There is no music of any sort on the soundtrack for well over two-thirds of its length, and often it is very unobtrusive. Lucas utilized the famous tune expertly, using it in its major key only twice (one of which is incomplete), but also using it in the minor key and in a variety of scorings to suggest danger, anticipation and risk. He also provided music of his own, not even distantly related to the Coates march, as backdrop to earlier scenes of the invention, testing, failure and eventual triumph of the bouncing-bomb. Holding back the major key march until 617 squadron sets off on the raid is a real masterstroke, for after many hints of it in dark, muted underscorings, its eventual appearance in its own colours provides an emotional release that matches perfectly the aircrews' own escape from weeks of waiting. It thus ties together audience and actors at a key moment. Though rarely dominant – it jars only in the brassy final version of the march as the credits roll, since by then the film has firmly eschewed triumphalism – Coates's march deserves its share of the film's immortality.

PROMOTION, RELEASE AND RECEPTION

A further cause of delay in releasing the picture arose because ABPC were determined to extract maximum attention from a film that promised both public attention and good business, especially after the delays in post-production meant that they missed the deadline for submitting it to the selection committee for the Royal Film Performance of 1955; had it gone in on time it would almost certainly have been chosen. The eventual first showing on 16 May 1955 was the twelfth anniversary of the dams raid, a news 'peg' thought well worth waiting for. ABPC certainly left no stone unturned in the meantime to prepare the ground: there was, for example, an advertisement in newspapers and on the hoardings during spring 1955 that won prizes on its own account – it won the 'poster of the month' award in *Today's Cinema*. It showed a sky empty except for three Lancaster bombers banking across the right-hand side, captioned as, 'The Dam Busters are coming'. The captive audience of film fans who read the *ABC Film Review* were not neglected either, with a story about the film in almost every monthly issue between April 1954 and September 1955.

Meanwhile the media were also being bombarded with such press releases as 'A great book becomes a great film', which proudly announced that Paul Brickhill's 'famous book ... one of the best-sellers of all time', a book which 'has been translated into practically every living language', was about to hit the screen.[6] Readers were reminded of the extreme technical difficulty of making such a film, but were reassured that 'high ranking RAF personnel' who had viewed it 'were unanimous in their opinion: "THE DAM BUSTERS" was a triumphant success!' Press releases banged on about the production 'sticking to the facts', and Anderson's ruling that there must be 'authenticity and accuracy'. They also reminded the press that Group Captain Whitworth had been both station commander at RAF Scampton in 1943 and technical adviser to the film, and so 'was able to provide valuable ... information which could only be given by one who had been on hand at the time. Where humanly possible, the film has faithfully reproduced every absorbing detail of the fantastic story of the breaching of the Ruhr dams.' This very specific claim raises an interesting if trivial question: if Whitworth had the valuable input 'which could only be given by one who had been on hand at the time', why did he allow the film to show Gibson's batman Crosby having to tell his master that his dog had just been killed, when the other sources indicate that in 1943 he decided to perform this task himself? Come to that, why did he let the film claim that the dog had been run over by a careless motorist who did not even stop, when in fact the animal's actions had caused the injury of the car-driver and his passenger as he desperately tried to avoid hitting it? The obvious answer is that compromises were made for dramatic effect, but that is hardly the impression that Associated British gave in 1955. Nor would they have liked to publish what Robert Clark was then writing to Barnes Wallis, that the film was a 'somewhat simplified treatment of highly complicated issues', necessarily so: there had to be some 'over-simplification because we have so little time to make clear to an uninstructed audience ... our film cannot hold interest unless we present "living" people whose feelings an audience can share', hence 'the many personal touches (by tacit admission fictional) introduced to this end'. This is an entirely reasonable way to defend any film on a historical subject, but most would not also claim with such insistence to be historically precise. In public, Clark would not have allowed the word 'fictional' to be associated with the film in any context at all. If those remarks from Clark to Wallis followed an objection from Wallis himself, he had the good sense to swallow his reservations and endorse the film. He was, after all, the person most to benefit from the fictionalization of 1943.

So many were the privileged guests that ABPC wished to associate with the film's release that it staged two separate royal premières at the Empire Theatre, Leicester Square, on 16 and 17 May 1955; a press release claimed that it was 'believed to be the first time in film history that a double "Premiere" in the West End has taken place on successive nights'. The first was in the presence of Princess Margaret, the second the Duke and Duchess of Gloucester, the Duchess of Gloucester being the vice-patron of the RAF Benevolent Fund, the Duke the president of Christ's Hospital Foundationers' Fund, another of the charities due to benefit from the première. The link with Christ's Hospital presumably arose from the fact that when Barnes Wallis was eventually given an award of £10,000 for his war-related inventions, he donated the money to his old school to fund the attendance there of RAF orphans. Asked to explain why he had not kept the money he had both fought for and deserved, he offered only a biblical reference to II Samuel, 14–17. This has King David rejecting the offer of water from the Philistines: instead, 'he poured it out unto the Lord ... Be it far from me, O Lord. That I should do this; is not this the blood of men that went in peril of their lives?'[7] By 1954, he was merely telling Laurence Thompson that 'anyone would feel deeply moved to feel responsible for the deaths of 60 young men'. Wallis was also quoted in 1954 as saying that 'if this film is made for the enduring glory of the Royal Air Force, it has number one priority with me'. Eric Coates likewise was quoted in 1955 as saying that his march was 'a kind of personal tribute to the men who bombed the Mohne dam of the Ruhr and to the RAF for their part in defeating Hitler's Germany'.[8]

The two premières included a march past by the Air Training Corps band, music in the theatre foyer by the RAF Central Band, and official attendance by such veterans' bodies as the RAF Escaping Society and the Pathfinder Association. One reason for two premières was the fact that both the RAF and the film industry wished to attend in force, and the mixing together of war veterans and film people both in reports of the events and in press photographs helpfully reinforced the filmmakers' claim that they had recorded actual history. ABPC's press release spoke of the event being attended by 'Statesmen, High-Ranking Officials of

Military and Civil Air Forces from all over the world, Britain's leading pilots, NATO Chiefs, and famous personalities representing science and the arts'. For once, the PR men were not exaggerating. As well as the film's cast and production personnel, there were also present surviving members of 617 squadron, the next of kin of its wartime casualties, Guy Gibson's family and friends, Barnes Wallis and his family, and all the wartime and post-war leaders of the RAF, including the Secretary of State for Air and Air Marshal Lord Tedder. Such was demand for tickets, that the first première was sold out within twenty-four hours, and the second was equally well attended when the time came. All of this attracted considerable media attention, including newsreel coverage by *Pathé News* on the première, valuable free publicity, not entirely unrelated, one suspects, to the fact that it was Associated British-Pathé that distributed the film in Europe and the UK.

Once the premières had been so successfully stage-managed, the company swung into a more familiar gear to impress the trade and the press. A two-page, colour brochure received wide circulation, two press-books were distributed (the larger for national and major regional papers, the smaller for local and weekly papers). These presented much the same case, arguing the film's authenticity in faithfully portraying a great act of British heroism and ingenuity, the public appetite for it demonstrated by Brickhill's book, and stills from the film as well as photographs of the original figures alongside their screen reincarnations. The larger version of the pressbook also incorporated plenty of photographs of those royal premières – not only such obvious moments as leading actors meeting Princess Margaret and war veterans shaking hands with the Duke of Gloucester, but also staged photographs of veterans of 617 squadron grouped around a model of the Mohne dam – with Barnes Wallis and Richard Todd both in attendance (once again linking, or confusing, the real thing and its cinematic portrayal).

For the distributing trade and small cinema-owners, ABPC had already laid on a large number of private showings around the country during April: Cardiff on the 19th, Liverpool on the 22nd, Glasgow on the 27th, and so on. It had also produced, as was customary with big-budget films in that era, a campaigning handbook for cinema-owners and managers. This showed the posters, handbills, stills and advertising material that would be available to cinemas booking the film, indicated contractual obligations in terms of relative type-sizes and specified wording for press advertisements, and described the 'national book tie-up' that had been arranged (Paul Brickhill's book was reprinted, with

display advertisements for the film to go into bookshops). More
deviously, managers were offered ready-made reviews that could be
inserted straight into local papers desperate for copy. So much was
relatively obvious, but the handbook also gave the regional and local
addresses of the RAF Association (veterans) and of the 'area publicists'
in the RAF's own regional offices, promising that they would do all they
could to help the film achieve the maximum audience (for example, by
putting posters in recruitment office windows). Managers were urged to
secure an RAF band to play on the local opening night for the film,
to get a guard of honour of ATC cadets for visiting dignitaries, even to
persuade the RAF to set up recruiting offices in cinema foyers and so
catch the young as they left the film (those foyers would already be
decorated with RAF crests, badges and mementoes), while outside the
doors the RAF could arrange for a plane to fly low overhead while an
army searchlight unit would pick it out in the night sky. Such elaborate
plans were by no means carried out everywhere, but local press archives
show enough positive examples of this advice being followed to demonstrate that what was going on in autumn 1955 in Britain was a great deal
of co-operation between Associated British Pictures and the RAF, for
mutual benefit. And if not every manager followed ABPC's advice,
others came up with stunts of their own; in Rugeley, Staffordshire, where
the cinema-manager won a special prize for his promotion of the film,
not only was there a recruiting office in the cinema, an ATC guard of
honour and fanfare trumpeters when civic leaders and local RAF officers
came to the opening night, but there was also a cake-making competition
involving most of the local bakers, all proceeds going to an RAF charity.

Much of this hype was probably unnecessary, for reviews of the film
itself would have produced long queues at the box-office when it finally
went on general release. The responses of film critics in the newspapers
and weeklies were nearly unanimous in their ungrudging praise. (Alan
Brien in the London *Evening Standard* was a rare exception, seeing the
film only as 'a near miss', and greatly disliking its special effects, though
the coup secured by the *Standard*'s rival, the *Evening News*, in serializing
Sherriff's script the same week may just possibly have put someone's
nose out of joint at the *Standard*. Needless to say, the *Evening News*
reviewer liked the film.) The reviewer in the third London evening
paper, the *Star*, concluded simply that 'if there has been a better war
film than *The Dam Busters* … then I must have missed it'.[9]

Among the biggest names in the reviewing trade, Dilys Powell,
C. A. Lejeune and William Whitebait were all distinctly impressed, as

they rarely were by 1950s war films. Powell in the *Sunday Times* (head-lined as 'Dam Busters' Glory') admitted to uncomfortable feelings when witnessing 'with whatever freedom from heat or malice, an event that brought major disaster to our late enemies', but added that 'once I have admitted to being aware of it I have made almost my only criticism of the film'. She hailed Michael Anderson as 'a new talent for the muted emotional scene', praising especially the restrained ending of the film, showing returning airmen 'with the exhausted look which one remembers on the face of returning airmen in wartime newsreels'. Powell also praised Sherriff's script, and the masterly use made by Anderson of silences (though 'understatement is never allowed to become the cliché that it often is in British films of this kind'), she liked Richard Todd's Gibson ('a likeable portrait of easy authority and coolness; it is well done, and it is enough') and thought Redgrave's Barnes Wallis the best thing he had done since *The Browning Version*. There was, though, just a hint of dissatisfaction in the final sentences: 'The girls, by the way, are scarcely seen in this single-minded film; only one or two waitresses and WRAFs, and one small women's role, that of the inventor's wife, pleas-antly played by Ursula Jeans.'[10]

Caroline Lejeune in the *Observer*, like Powell and Whitebait, devoted most of her weekly column to this one film. She thought that the film might be overlong in the raid sequences, but admitted that the audience had found those same sequences enthralling, and she had shared Wallis's elation when the dams were finally breached. She hinted that Todd's Gibson 'may not be the real Gibson', but accepted that 'he suggests a fine type, the sort of leader to whom loyalty seems reasonable'. Lejeune too liked Anderson's direction and Sherriff's 'beautifully simple script', and, having offered a few cavils, concluded, 'but make no mistake, this is a fine and memorable film'. Whitebait thought that 'the film takes its time but its problem [how to bomb the dams] always engrosses'. He regretted the taming down of some of the sharper moments from Brick-hill's book, such as Bomber Harris greeting Wallis with, 'What the hell do you want? I've no time for you damned inventors.' In the film he had become 'a sort of father-figure, like the Stalin of Russian films'. But Whitebait of the *New Statesman* did 'not want to seem exacting about a film that obviously achieves its purpose ... *The Dam Busters* tells its story plainly, and makes effective use of pauses: the long moments before setting out and the aftermath, with a BBC report going on and the survivors sitting down to breakfast among empty tables'.[11]

The *Daily Telegraph*'s man seemed to have stuck closely to ABPC's pressbook for information, but he paid glowing testimony to the film's ability to produce tension and audience involvement even in a story where everyone already knew the ending. 'Though in such an epic there can be no surprise, though one knows in an abstract second-hand way just what is coming, it is still impossible not to feel the heart beat faster as the planes skim over Holland and climb the Ruhr hills.' He, like most reviewers, had no doubt that the actual raid of 1943 had been a great success, and had indeed been 'a mission that possibly did more than any other to win the war in the West'. Believing that about the raid, and seeing the film as an honest and painstaking account of it, made it impossible for him not to view it too as an important and successful film. 'Michael Anderson has handled the trick stuff with skill and the emotion with restraint. As for the acting, the cast [wa]s so large and so excellent' that he had room only to single out Redgrave, Todd and Sydney for personal accolades. The *Financial Times* thought that the film had retold 'a stirring wartime deed of 12 years ago with restraint and painstaking documentary thoroughness. But its power to tug us back to the brave times it celebrates depends, perhaps, less upon art than upon its simple directness of approach.' Finally, among the quality press, the anonymous reviewer in *The Times* (headlined with what was for 'The Thunderer' in the 1950s an absolute rave: 'Film of Unusual Merit'), really went overboard. For this reviewer, all the films about the air war from *The Way to the Stars* onwards were, in comparison with *The Dam Busters*, 'as a caveman's scribblings on a wall to a Rembrandt'. Previously there had been no satisfactory example of 'the fiction-documentary formula, which is particularly our own', in any account of the bombers' war, but now, 'the last word has been said. Here is a full statement, final and complete.' The reviewer delighted in the script ('faultless'), the unhurried direction of Anderson, and the avoidance of 'artificial heroics' throughout. He also especially liked Redgrave's portrayal of Wallis; though more sceptical of Todd's Gibson he nevertheless decided that 'as an Academy portrait in an average year it would gain, and deserve, approval'.[12]

Among the less exalted newspapers, Derek Mounsey in the *Sunday Express* enthused, 'At Last! The Real War', and told his readers that he would certainly go to see the film again, referring more than once to the film's honesty and its 'semi-documentary' feel. 'This film *is* the war. It is real and true', and this, he thought, brought the film 'within reach of greatness'. Peter Burnup in the *News of the World* admitted that he had 'trembled' when he first heard of the plan to film the 1943 raid, but 'those qualms were unjustified', for 'the film climbs to clouds of glory which befit the RAF itself'. He was not alone in reviewing the film as if he was expected to pass judgement on the RAF rather than ABPC (which goes far to explain all that RAF involvement in publicizing the picture). 'You come away with the feeling that the RAF is the true hero. Go to this picture and be proud.' Likewise, the *Star* thought it was 'a picture without a blemish. It is thrilling. It is moving. It is true. And I think you should be proud to see it.' The *Daily Mail*'s Fred Majdalany thought it 'one of the best war pictures yet made', Paul Dehn in the *News Chronicle* called it 'the finest war picture', and Paul Holt of the *Daily Herald* 'the best since *The Cruel Sea*'. All praised Sherriff's script, Anderson's direction, and the acting of the leading players. Reg Whitley of the *Daily Mirror* ('Excuse me while I rave') thought it 'about the finest flying picture I've seen' (he also warned his readers that 'a black retriever dog, the C.O.'s pet, nearly steals the picture'). All of these also found the film to be moving, honest and true.[13]

The extent of the consensus among the critics is given added weight when it is realized that a Liberal paper like the *News Chronicle* and Labour supporters such as the *Mirror*, the *Herald* and the *New Statesman* were as vocal in their support for this rather conservative film as were the *Mail* and the *Express*. The reason for this is partly to be found in the quality of the film, but it also owed something to the fact that the war itself – and the 1943 raid as symbolic of the war effort – was still a recent event of which British people of every political stripe felt intensely proud. This was a British film, celebrating a purely British, or rather British Empire, victory, and one that manifestly owed nothing either to over-mighty allies like the USA or to under-mighty opponents like Italy. This is brought out clearly enough by the review that the film received in the communist *Daily Worker* ('Deathless war feat lives again … magnificently exciting picture'). It had no doubt that the raid itself 'played an appreciable part in defeating Nazi Germany', and was equally certain that this was 'straightforward, honest and remarkably fresh. It is a fine tribute to brave men that makes one forget the dozen or more shoddy essays on the same theme that have gone before.' This being the *Daily Worker*, things did not, however, rest there. A few days later, the paper printed a letter from F. L. Edwards of south-east London, expressing 'surprise' that a paper of the left would give a favourable review of 'the latest RAF recruiting film, *The Dam Busters*. No doubt it is technically well made, well acted and so forth; but surely we are not therefore obliged to overlook the fact that the film treats war as an adventure and, far worse, justifies the indiscriminate massacre of civilians?' Not so, responded the newspaper's critic, Thomas Spencer, for 'the breaching of the Mohne Dam struck a tremendous blow at Hitler's main war arsenal' (and British communists had been all in favour of fighting Hitler – at least from June 1941). Spencer loftily expressed incomprehension as to how 'a film which treats this episode in a straightforward way ... can be described as "an RAF recruiting film"', but his main argument rested on the premise that 'there was nothing indiscriminate about the bombing of the Mohne Dam, a carefully chosen and legitimate military target'. This confident pronouncement closed the correspondence, or at least the editor declined to print any more letters on the subject, but we may feel that F. L. Edwards had at least a near miss with his argument, given what we now know about the RAF's support for the film's promotion to the paying public (not to mention setting up recruitment desks in foyers).[14] The paper might also have had second thoughts when Michael Anderson duly won the C. P. Robertson Memorial Trophy for 'the best interpretation of the RAF in any field during 1955'. The point was that the raid did indeed represent an attempt to hit a specific military target, but when reviewers raved about the film as showing 'the real war', rather than a small part of it, they were doing the RAF as a whole a great service. Making this film at all – and especially when making it so well and so persuasively – when no company even thought of making a film about the fire-bombing of Hamburg or the destruction of Dresden, productions with which the RAF would surely *not* have been so co-operative, was in itself contributing to a skewed version of the recent war in the popular memory.

When we move from newspapers to more specialist film magazines, we get a further indication of the division that might have occurred among the more widely read reviewers – but didn't. As they were for most war films, the film journals were cool if not hostile, though most conceded that *The Dam Busters* was a better made and far more restrained film than most of the genre. *Films and Filming*'s John Minchinton accepted that this was 'a story of something that really influenced the last war' and liked its sticking to sober facts and avoiding glorification of either the events or the people. But he thought both the acting and the direction weak, lacking in 'the drama of character' that Brickhill had brought out in his book. What was honest in the film worked because the young men who had fought in 1939–45 had known what they were fighting for and what they were fighting against (the implication being that in the Cold War there were no such certainties), but the real thrust of the review was a call for equally large budgets now to be devoted to films that would hymn peace rather than war, for 'peace does not lack drama' (actually, of course, it does, and that was for people like Minchinton the whole problem). In a similar vein, the British Film Institute's *Monthly Listing* praised technical qualities in the film but then added fairly dismissively that *The Dam Busters* was 'based firmly on the conventions built up over the years by the British war film' (and regular readers would have known exactly how bad that made it).[15]

If we look at trade papers, we find that they were even more euphoric about the film than the daily press. Their duty was specifically to advise on saleability, and of that they had no doubt whatsoever, using throughout the enthusiastic tone of voice that a producer would most wish to read in reviews of his film. *Today's Cinema* had no word of criticism: dialogue 'has the genuine service flavour'; black and white was 'eminently suitable for the subject'; Redgrave's acting was 'a masterly piece of observation'; it 'could almost be called a documentary, in that it is a scrupulously factual, unvarnished account of an actual event. It has not been "dramatised" in the sense of having fictional detail added. But director Anderson wisely lets the heroic story speak for itself. Nothing is emphasised. Nothing is underlined.' Most importantly for a cinema manager with an eye on the box-office: 'though completely without romantic interest, and with only the lightest leavenings of humour, this is a film with all the other attributes of box office success, particularly with ex-service patrons. It is exciting, absorbing and inspiring, and should be a deservedly profitable booking for all popular situations.'[16]

Much the same advice came from *Kinematograph Weekly*, its summary of the 'box-office angle' of the film being 'outstanding British booking and must for all types of hall' (helpfully adding 'excellent for children', so extending the sale of tickets to family parties too). In the text ('Reviews for Showmen'), Josh Billings perceptively argued that 'the film is sure to make a terrific impact at the box office while at the same time earning a place in the archives'. The review waxed lyrical, quoting Winston Churchill at one point to suggest how much the country owed 'to the bomber boys', as if it was everyone's duty to go and see the film for this reason too. He listed its 'points of appeal' as 'inspiring real-life story, grand acting, resourceful, sensitive and showmanlike direction, spellbinding highlights, powerful patriotic angle and box-office [bestselling book] title'. What more could a manager want than a guarantee that he could do his patriotic duty and make a profit too?[17]

THE DAM BUSTERS AT THE BOX-OFFICE AT HOME
AND ABROAD

Billings was exactly right in his prediction of the film's commercial appeal, and his own January 1956 annual survey of films' performance at the box-office duly placed *The Dam Busters* as the top-grossing film of the previous year, though it had gone on general release only in September and was still showing in some places at the start of 1956. Vincent Porter's analysis of the British box-office performance of releases by ABPC, Warners, MGM and British Lion makes the point admirably: *The Dam Busters* was 'a soaraway financial success'. Its initial release secured bookings in 467 cinemas, almost all for at least a full week, when hardly any other ABPC or British Lion film of the decade managed more than 300 (and it was more typical for a third or a half of the bookings to be for only three days). Since about two-thirds of cinemas that booked the film were independents, rather than part of ABPC's own chain, the campaign to persuade managers and owners was clearly effective. The film took £552,687 at the box-office in the first year, so recovering its costs before much of the foreign exhibition had even begun and long before its periodic re-releases and television showings added to the profits. By comparison, other successful war films such as *Odette*, *Angels One Five* and *The Wooden Horse* collected only about half as much in gross receipts, as did such notable films of the period as *The Third Man* and *The African Queen*.[18]

The film's performance on first release in Sheffield was fairly typical for a provincial city. Initially it was announced with considerable advance publicity for the Hippodrome cinema, one of the two or three city-centre locations that got big films first; here the advertisements noted 'Free List Suspended', so that tradesmen who usually got free tickets in return for putting posters in their windows would not do so this time, since there would be no empty seats. The film was first shown on Monday, 12 September, and then, most unusually for this cinema, held over for a second week. A review in the *Sheffield Telegraph* proudly noted that the actual 'Busters' had practised in the Derwent Valley, which provided the city with some of its water ('Sheffield patrons have a special interest in the film being shown this week') and reported packed houses. (Partly because of a misrecollection by Gibson in his autobiography, this dam became for Brickhill and the film 'Derwentwater', which is in the Lake District and does not have a dam.) A fortnight after the film closed at the Hippodrome, it reopened for a week's run at the Abbeydale and Wicker cinemas, locations just outside the city centre, but still well-appointed cinemas which got films fairly early after release, and in both cases it ran for a week rather than the usual three days. Before the end of the year, it had trickled down to the Essoldo and Forum cinemas, both in working-class suburbs where admission prices would be cheaper and comfort much less, though still running for a full week in each case, which suggests that audience demand was holding up well. Not until 1956 did it reach rural Bakewell. By March 1956 the film had been shown at about a dozen cinemas in the Sheffield area. It is a commentary on the ubiquity of British war films in the mid-1950s that in the same weeks in which Sheffielders first went to see *The Dam Busters*, the local cinemas were also showing *The Colditz Story*, *The Ship That Died of Shame*, and (on re-release) *In Which We Serve*.[19] Back in 1943, Charles Whitworth, when he received 617 squadron's groundstaff at Scampton, had reminded them of *In Which We Serve* and the answer to Noël Coward's question as to what made an efficient ship, which was 'a happy ship'. Scampton, he assured them, would be just such a team. The juxtaposition of art and life in the mind of the man who was both 617 squadron's station commander and *The Dam Busters*' technical adviser was, it seems, seamless. And so was the influence of war films on the British public.

It was not only in Sheffield that local press reviews echoed those from Fleet Street and it is clear that the film's appeal to the public repeatedly caused it to be held over for additional weeks when the initial booking had failed to satisfy local demand. Much the same happened when the film was shown in Canada, Australia and New Zealand, where reviews were favourable and business very good. In Toronto, Montreal and Ottawa, Richard Todd was deluged with personal appearances, interviews and civic receptions, on one occasion racing through Toronto's traffic lights with a police motor-cycle escort, so as to make appearances at two cinemas which were showing the film at almost the same time on the same evening.

In Australia, the film opened in Melbourne with a gala 'invitation-only' première in the presence of the Governor of Victoria and of the five Australian survivors of 617 squadron, reviewers happily noting the local significance of the story and reclaiming the story as part of Australia's own war. The première programme was based on that for the London events, but was customized for Melbourne with a foreword by the Chief of the Australian Air Staff, and by adding to the usual page which showed Todd as Gibson and Redgrave as Wallis a photograph of Nigel Stock as Spafford (rather an odd choice this, since Stock was British, while Bill Kerr was an Australian himself as well as playing an

Australian in the film). The film played for over a month in a large Melbourne cinema, and then for several weeks in the suburbs, doing equally well in both Sydney and Perth, where the première again attracted the state governor, senior politicians and airmen. It remains a film familiar to Australians, now mainly as in Britain through video and approximately annual television exposure on the ABC. It has retained the same currency in Canada, where Michael Anderson now lives; he finds that it is easily the best-known of his films there.

Only half the pilots of 617 squadron were Britons: along with the single American, the rest came from Canada, Australia and New Zealand. The squadron's aircrew were rather similar: 'Norm' Barlow's crew, for example, contained two Australians, a Canadian and four Britons, all of whom died on the raid, while the groundstaff were memorably described by an NCO as a collection of 'Rhodesians, Canadians, Scots, Welsh, Geordies and English (sic)'. The film, in the accents heard throughout mess and briefing scenes, and more directly in the foregrounding of Bill Kerr's Mickey Martin, had been faithful to the original. This can have done no harm when playing to audiences in the Dominions, whose newspapers had in 1943 proudly highlighted their own men's contributions. Adelaide in South Australia furnishes a good example of this. In 1943, the original story of the raid ran for five successive days in the local press, with special interest being taken in Spafford and Shannon, the two South Australians who had been on the raid, culminating with an interview with Spafford, who spoke of Gibson as 'a marvellous pilot', and recounted his deliberate drawing of enemy fire. In 1956, the *Advertiser* duly retrod all this ground, telling its readers that Spafford's name was now to be found on the state war memorial as a war hero, so establishing a local share in the ownership of *The Dam Busters*, which duly ran for almost two months in the city.[20]

The British Empire flavour of the film may indeed explain why *The Dam Busters* 'bombed' in the United States (a quite irresistible pun). For Richard Todd this was once again a case of Associated British proving to be too mean for their own good, failing to promote the film properly in the world's largest market and so failing to harvest the potential rewards. Going on to Hollywood from Toronto and finding to his amazement that nobody there seemed to have noticed the recent runaway success of his best film, he got hold of a print and showed it to Darryl F. Zanuck, Dana Wynter and other Hollywood friends. When the film ended, Zanuck 'rasped' out 'Gee! That's one hell of a picture! Is that a true story?' When Todd replied, 'Absolutely', he responded, 'Then why doesn't it say so?' There had of course been no need to 'say so' in Britain, but Todd 'saw his point', and thereafter tried to persuade Associated British to step up its marketing of the film, perhaps by getting either Winston Churchill (who absolutely loved the film) or Dwight Eisenhower to endorse it as a true record of a heroic event, in a specially recorded prologue.[21] He had no success, possibly because Robert Clark had already read the American trade reviews which ranged only from the unenthusiastic to the downright hostile. *Variety* had decided as early as June 1955 that this was a worthy release with significance for Britain but little for anyone else:

> As a record of a British operational triumph during the last war, *The Dam Busters* will be hard to beat. This is a small slice of history, told in painstaking detail and overflowing with the British quality of understatement. The documentary-like quality increases its appeal and this should be no barrier to sturdy box office results in most situations. This has the makings of a box office success at home and should notch healthy returns in overseas territories.

This was hardly the stuff to get cinema-managers in the USA (which certainly did not think of itself as a British 'overseas territory') reaching for their chequebooks, and later paragraphs praising the technical skills of the actors, editors and model-builders did nothing to repair the damage. In the same way, Jack Moffitt in the *Hollywood Reporter* had headlined his review unpromisingly as 'British Production is Off Beaten Track'. He argued that nobody had tried to make a film about an inventor since the failure of *Dr Ehrlich's Magic Bullet* – though the cure for venereal disease was not exactly similar to the bouncing-bomb, and he never told his readers that this was actually a war film. He also laboriously pointed out the film's problems with American viewers, for example the fact that Richard Todd was the only actor of whom they would have heard, and then administered the *coup de grâce*: 'because it contains no love story, it may be difficult to sell to the American public. Yet, a typical audience at the [Los Angeles] preview followed the movie with keen attention and rewarded it with spontaneous applause. As always, with something different, the problem will be to get them in.'[22]

Nobody would base a commercial decision to book the film on such a trade review, whatever it said about the rest of the film. It was notable that Moffitt felt the necessity to spend most of his review telling the film's story – something that no British reviewer needed to do – and this may explain a great deal about the different commercial fortunes of the film in America and Britain. Michael Anderson points out that the very title of the film, *The Dam Busters*, so evocative in the Commonwealth, conveyed little or nothing to Americans. The *Motion Picture Herald* also damned with faint praise, rating it only as 'good' when really successful releases all got 'very good' or 'excellent': 'This is a story about men dedicated to country, but as is usual in a British picture, without obvious heroics.' The review was not an impressive piece of writing, confusing books by Gibson and Brickhill and stating erroneously that 617 squadron had not been formed to attack the Ruhr dams, but was nearer the point in concluding that the film's makers 'have not leavened this with the comic relief which in American films is trite but somehow needed'. Overall, it was 'a man's film', and then mainly for those interested in technical issues relating to flying, not for the public at large. 'To others, considering the story is about a World War II military effort which at the time meant little to the American reading audience, the distance in time and even in outlook may seem too great; and the intense single-minded preparation for fearsome death and the continual noise on the soundtrack too unpleasant.'[23]

Stung by criticism in the British press, ABPC claimed in press releases that their film was being 'intensively promoted' in the USA, but neither ABPC nor their American distributor Warner Brothers bought space in the trade papers to advertise *The Dam Busters* and so counter such negative reviews. It is at least possible, as Richard Todd believed, and as Jack Moffitt hinted in describing audience reactions at the LA preview, that Americans would have liked the film if only they had been given a chance to see it. But this is not likely, for in places like New York where the film was actually shown (though not reviewed in the city's papers), 'word of mouth' did not save it either. It closed early in Brooklyn, the cinema-manager explaining that 'the public is tired of war films', in marked contrast to the public demand which kept it showing in Britain.

Considering how little business it was getting in the USA, it seems hard on Associated British that *The Dam Busters* caused them so much trouble there. Not only did they have to claim that they were indeed trying to promote it, despite evidence to the contrary, but they also ran into severe trouble when the American version was doctored by Warners to make it exciting enough for Americans. They could hardly add a sub-plot with a love theme or increase the quota of jokes. They could, though, try to make the action more gripping by showing more planes crashing in flames, and since they did not have stockshots of crashing Lancasters in the archives, they did the best they could with old material showing the crash of a Flying Fortress. Unfortunately, this somehow came to light in Britain, and as a result questions were asked in the House of Commons and highly indignant articles appeared in the press. The gist of all this irritation was that it was almost sacrilegious to tamper with the film's truthfulness – but beneath the surface there were strong implications that the Americans were somehow trying to steal a British victory and make it their own. Interestingly, when in the 1990s American filmmakers did indeed steal British Second World War exploits for their domestic audiences (capture of the Enigma codebook), strong rumours immediately circulated that Hollywood would now remake *The Dam Busters*, probably with Gibson and Wallis as Americans. As in 1955, the British response was a strong and indignant 'How dare they?' The way in which such anger illustrated the British determination to *own* the Dam Busters as an exclusively British property goes far to explain why Americans did not wish to see the 1955 film. It is easy enough to see how the film *might* have been constructed from the start to appeal to a wider American public – more overt heroics, better known (and preferably American) stars, the building up of the one actual American in 617 squadron, Joe McCarthy from Coney Island, and some love interest centred on Dinghy Young and his Californian wife. The result, of course, would have been outrage, fury and protest in Britain (and possibly even failure at the box-office there). It was impossible to have it both ways, but this did not prevent the British press from trying, and the episode of the 'Flying Fortress' did at least prompt *The Times* to one of its own finest hours in pomposity, smugness and latent anti-Americanism. It editorialized as follows:

A Film Extra

Just on ten years after MR. ERROL FLYNN liberated Burma for the delectation of American film audiences, it has been revealed that they have also had their morale uplifted – and perhaps the box-offices enriched – by the suggestion that the United States had something to do with the blowing up of the Mohne dam. *The Times* critic said it was 'a full statement, final and complete'. But the distributors of the film in a rather unresponsive American market sought, it seems, to improve on finality. So they joined an American Flying Fortress, pathetically out of formation, to the historic and heroic nineteen. They now plead that the incursion was, like the baby in *Mr. Midshipman Easy*, only a little one: a matter of a mere two seconds' glimpse. That was apparently considered enough to satisfy the Walter Mittys in the audience. And now, following the hubbub, even that has been taken out. Tampering with history is always serious, and *The Dam Busters* was made rather as a documentary film than as a piece of entertainment. This effort to improve on it was childish and silly. But now that publicity has been given to the matter it would be equally childish if we in Britain got too indignant about it. The subject was raised in Parliament last Wednesday – a protest to America was asked for – but even though the UNDER-SECRETARY OF STATE FOR AIR said he would consider what action, if any, to take, the sensible answer is silence. Most Americans will feel the episode was an insult to their intelligence and will be angry with whatever has made them, as a nation, seem ridiculous. We can well afford to let it go at that.[24]

Rather more seriously, the American version had stripped out all the documentary-like scenes of the film, such as the silent moments in barrack-rooms before the raid and again when it is over, what Michael Anderson regards as 'the emotional heart of the film'. In doing so Warners were no doubt speeding up a slow narrative of understatement to suit American tastes, but they were also weakening tremendously the whole film, and this cannot have helped in the American market either. But there may be little that needs explaining when we assess the failure of *The Dam Busters* in the USA. Few British films managed to make money in the American market in the 1950s, and the Rank Organisation indeed lost a fortune trying to break through. British war films generally did badly there, unless like, say, *The Bridge on the River Kwai* or *The Battle of the River Plate*, they were really international productions anyway, and had all the box-office appeal that *The Dam Busters* lacked – international (and American) stars, glamour and love interest, a reasonable amount of humour, and colourful locations shot on colour film. Those few exceptions rather proved the rule. If this was hard for British filmmakers to accept – Kenneth More, for example, fumed in his autobiography that *Reach for the Sky* had failed in America mainly because it was set at a time in which Britain was fighting for its life while America was still neutral – then they had only themselves to blame.[25] The more that films like *The Dam Busters* strove to be accurate depictions of Britain's own war and celebrations of exclusively British victories, the less they were likely to be welcome in Chicago or St Louis. In 1953, before filming even started, *The Dam Busters*' production manager had already noted in his diary that 'it is a very doubtful proposition in the American and Continental markets', which meant that the filmmakers would have its maximize its appeal to the home market in order to get back their investment, but this in turn made it inherently less saleable in the USA. When *The Dam Busters* was shown to one group of American distributors and cinema-managers in 1955, three-quarters of them voted it 'poor' or 'below average', and only two out of forty rated it 'good'. One of those present wrote that he found it hard to believe that his customers would want to see a film in which 'a bunch of guys with limey accents' acted as if they were saving the world. There's no reason to think that American showmen were worse judges of their customers' likes and dislikes than their British counterparts.

THE AFTER-LIFE OF A FILM

A film as successful as *The Dam Busters* had been at the British box-office would not be allowed to fade from the memory. Before the end of the 1950s it had been re-released for further tours of the British circuits and after its first premature re-release late in 1956 seems again to have managed to do good business. Smaller suburban and rural cinemas were still showing it during the 1960s, as was the Classic cinema chain, and (in 16mm format) so were schools and cinema clubs. When home video-recorders became popular from the 1970s, it was rapidly released for home viewing in video format, has remained available for almost the whole period since, and was specially re-released in a fiftieth anniversary VHS edition in May 1993 – the anniversary not of the film but of the raid.

It was indeed its conquest of the small screen that really ensured its immortality as a film, and in the process entrenched the lasting popular fame of the raid too. Since the film industry rightly perceived television to be a threat to its commercial viability, it was at first reluctant to sell on its products to a rival, while television was until the 1960s more anxious to establish its own capability as a medium of entertainment than to show old stock from the cinemas. Gradually however, as the film companies became more desperate to realize the capital tied up in half a century of old films, and as television strove to fill the schedules of more channels and longer broadcasting hours, a convergence of self-interest emerged and allowed films to be reshown on television, though at first it was mainly American films, and the British companies insisted that only older and less successful films could be shown. *The Dam Busters* was therefore one of the first important British films to be shown on the televisions of the nation, premièring in an 'All Time Greats' season, on Sunday 4 February 1973, on BBC1 at the peak time of 8.15 p.m. This was a big coup for the BBC, meriting special attention in the *Radio Times*: the blurb describing 'this famous British film', Willis Hall's column made it one of the 'my choice' programmes of the week (even though scheduled against *The Goodies* on BBC2), while Philip Jenkinson wrote that 'it makes absorbing stuff', and likened its cast to 'a *Who's Who* of 50s British cinema'. It also received a new round of appreciative reviews from the newspapers' television critics, Cecil Williams in the *Daily Mail* for example calling it 'one of the most stirring of all war films'. It was agreed that transition to the small screen had been a success, that the screen ratio and black-and-white format of the original film had worked well at a time when domestic televisions were much the same, and that it would be far from the last time that TV would show the film.

It has been shown almost annually in Britain ever since, and, though its place in the schedules has slipped gradually from peak hours to late evenings and weekday afternoons, even a BBC reshowing in 1982 generated a special article in *The Listener* ('Everyone knows the story...'). Its constant repetition proves that it continues to command an audience, increasingly an audience who can never have seen the film in a cinema and most of whom can have had few other sources of information about the 1943 raid. It has also remained even after half a century a film for the memorial occasion, with a special showing timed to coincide with the fiftieth anniversary of the raid and another fifty years after VE day. The fact that *The Dam Busters* was a film made ten years after the war, while others then shown were actually made in wartime, occasioned little comment, so completely were the raid and the film viewed as a single entity by then – as the BBC showed clearly enough when they used extracts from *the film* to illustrate a news bulletin on that fiftieth anniversary of the raid in 1993, without using the usual caption to indicate that these were not actuality pictures of the event. Writing in *Classic Television* in 1997, Martin Jackson reviewed the whole genre of 1950s war films which had made such an impact on television over a quarter of a century, and concluded that '*The Dam Busters* is certainly the most famous of all British war films', its story of bouncing-bombs and low-flying bombers irresistible 'boys-own stuff'. Its message, he thought, as in most of the genre, was that 'it is teamwork and comradeship which pulls people through'.[26] How far, though, have messages conveyed by the film been influential? Here, of course, we must bear in mind that its influence was only as part of a package, as one of the best – probably *the* best – of the British war films of the 1950s which had many common characteristics. Films of the genre also need to be evaluated alongside the books that spawned them. Brickhill's *The Dam Busters* is still in print in 2002, the film is available on video and Coates's march on several CDs.

The film conveyed a sense of British skill, superiority and ingenuity that was intensely reassuring at the time it was made, but not entirely helpful in the long run. George Baker recalls how much the British people in the mid-1950s, only just emerging from the disappointments of post-war austerity, needed a film like *The Dam Busters* to enable them to take pride in winning the war. As Winston Churchill told his constituents in 1952, his 'faith [wa]s unbroken in the strength, genius, and inexhaustible resourcefulness of the British race', within which race he undoubtedly included the men of the Dominions, exactly the reassurance that the filmscript then in preparation was going to convey. At the time of the film's release Churchill had just, at last, retired and he left a huge gap in British public life. Michael Anderson remembers the British need for a hero at that time, and that Richard Todd and Michael Redgrave in their very different ways filled that gap, part of his explanation for the film's huge impact. (He might have added, from outside the world of films, 'brave Don Cockell', whose defeat by Rocky Marciano in a world heavyweight championship fight was reported on the same day as *The Dam Busters* première in many papers. Cockell was even then being added to a long line of British sporting heroes whose fame derived from embodying the Dunkirk spirit, resourcefulness and guts in adversity.)

The film also carries certain social messages – the leadership of the elite, the insignificance of women, the essential priority of 'character' over caution and hard work in fighting life's battles – which may well have been positively harmful in building up dangerous stereotypes. For Richard Morris, it extolled 'the golden age of British individualism, witnessed in brilliant improvisation, casually laconic dialogue, and the cool bravado of confident men. Today much of it seems risible, but golden ages are ultimately created not by authors but by audiences that need them. The interest of *The Dam Busters* lies not only in the tale but in the manner of its telling.'[27]

And influential it certainly was. The young Peter Chapman (author of the inimitable *The Goalkeeper's History of Britain*), for example, who grew up in Islington in the 1950s, was shattered to find when he watched his first televised international football match in 1956 (in the same stadium, be it noted, where Hitler had attended the 1936 Olympics), that the Germans had *scored* against England, and (though they lost 3–1) cheered as if this was a hugely important moment:

There was nothing in my cultural heritage to prepare me for the fact that the Germans might win. None of my comics, nor any film I had seen, had anything but a recurrent collection of Fritzes leering their way towards comfortable victory, ultimately beaten by their deficiency of character. When down, we got up, bounced bombs on water, sent in pilots on tin legs, or chased their battleships to distant Norwegian fjords and harbours in Latin America. We might have a tendency to get in tight situations ourselves – trapped on narrow beaches for example – but it only needed a chirpy British private to wave a thumbs-up at the encircling Germans and say 'Not 'arf', for them to rush out with hands aloft yelling, '*Kamerad! Kamerad!*'[28]

Note the centrality of films in this teenage sense of the national identity, and note that his first example is drawn – as it *must* be – from *The Dam Busters*. In much the same way, Peter Hennessy, as so often speaking in the first person plural for the same generation of late-1940s baby-boomers, recently reminisced that 'we spent the fifties in cinemas absorbing an endless diet of war films in which Richard Todd and Kenneth More convinced us that there is a singular mixture of insouciance, bravery and flair that we [British] could bring to the conduct of international affairs'. As Hennessy hints, this was not an uncomplicated set of emotional baggage to drag with us into the second half of the century.[29]

Although, in the year after *The Dam Busters* premièred, the Suez crisis proved to the discerning that the British Empire no longer wore any clothes as a great power (*The Dam Busters* was in fact first appearing in Australia in that same week), British public opinion, British tabloid newspapers, and many British politicians have remained amazingly oblivious of the fact. How else to explain the national myopia about 'Europe', how else the rage whenever Germany wins a football game, or the national euphoria when 'we' beat 'them'. Football may indeed have replaced warfare as the pitch on which Britain's contests with Germany were played in the second half of the twentieth century, but we need to recall that the few critics who disliked *The Dam Busters* and other war films of the time did so precisely because they seemed to portray warfare and national rivalry as 'just a game'. Ironically, when Margaret Thatcher tried in 1990 to console cabinet colleagues for Britain's defeat by Germany in the World Cup, remarking brightly that 'It's only a game' and provoking a minister to respond despairingly, 'But, it's our national game', she allegedly replied, 'Never mind. We've beaten them at their national game twice this century.' This was not a new joke (it went back to the 1940s), but it was still significant on the lips of one who rarely made jokes, and who was privately concerned at just that time lest German unification allow Helmut Kohl to establish a German domination of Europe where Hitler had failed. She was by no means alone in such views.

There were, after all, *two* television advertisements for beer in the late 1980s that depended on a knowledge of the dam-busting raid of 1943. The one that did *not* win a prize in the 2000 television viewers' vote involves a tall, bronzed Englishman, somewhat reminiscent of Roger Moore as 007, emerging on to the balcony of a Mediterranean resort, spotting with amusement a group of fat Germans waddling to the best places around the pool (all looking like overweight Gert Frobes in *Goldfinger*). He effortlessly throws his rolled-up union-jack towel so that it bounces several times on the water before neatly unrolling on the best lounger at the far end of the pool – as the big tune plays on the soundtrack. It hardly needs saying that there were several protests in Germany over the screening of such unhelpfully negative images of an ally's national identity, or that the British tabloids reassured their readers that this merely proved that Germans had no sense of humour (as we had always known – partly because of war films). With what outrage would the same tabloids have reacted if they had remembered that German propagandists had in 1943 denounced the dams raid as a war crime against civilians, or that in 1955 German papers had regretted the making of a film that would merely add to 'the glorification of a gruesome act' and sniffily refused to allow location shooting over the Mohne dam?

The dams raid is certainly not remembered as a gruesome act by the British, rather as a consummate act of skill, bravery and sacrifice in a good cause – but these are after all not incompatible reactions to the same military event. In shaping that popular memory, and in ensuring that the raid has stayed in the popular memory, *The Dam Busters* film was clearly, for good or ill, a key influence. But when all the analysis is over, it remains necessary to restate the central fact about that film: it remains, fifty years after being made, a film that is treasured because it is still so watchable, enjoyable and (for British and Commonwealth audiences, anyway) involving, moving and exhilarating. Of very few British films of that vintage can this be said. Australian Foreign Minister Richard Casey was not speaking only for his own countrymen when he noted in his diary in May 1955: 'We went to *The Dam Busters* film late today. I think it is the most tremendous film that I've ever seen.'[30]

Notes

INTRODUCTION

1. Sweetman, *The Dambusters Raid*.
2. King-Smith, *The Fox Busters*.

1. THE HISTORICAL BACKGROUND

1. *Argus*, Melbourne, 21 May 1953.
2. Sweetman, *The Dambusters Raid*, pp. 161–3.
3. Richards and St George Saunders, *Royal Air Force 1939–1945: Vol. 2*, p. 296.
4. Sweetman, *The Dambusters Raid*, pp. 2, 73–6, 80–1, 125–46.
5. Ibid., pp. 181–4.
6. This is the view both of 617 squadron veterans interviewed for the BBC television documentary, *The Dambusters* (1993), and of the more official narration of the RAF Museum's video *Dambusters, the True Story* (1993).
7. Jackson, 'Black and White Army'.
8. Harris, *Bomber Offensive*, p. 158.
9. *New York Times*, 18 May 1943.
10. Sweetman, *The Dambusters Raid*, p. 175.
11. Ottaway, *Dambuster*, p. 138; Morris, *Guy Gibson*, p. 221.
12. Gibson, *Enemy Coast Ahead*, pp. 255–6.
13. Ibid., p. 188.
14. Ibid., p. 8.
15. Ibid., p. 7.
16. Ibid., pp. 140–1.
17. *Daily Telegraph*, 8 February 1946; *Times Literary Supplement*, 9 March 1946; Harris, *Bomber Offensive*, p. 158.
18. *The Times*, 26 April 1991.
19. Brickhill, *The Dam Busters*, p. 9.
20. Alexander Gibson to Robert Clark, 2 October 1954, BFI *Dam Busters* micro-jacket.
21. *Daily Telegraph*, 8 February 1946.
22. Brickhill, *The Dam Busters*, p. 9.

23. Frankland, *History at War*, p. 179; Morris, *Guy Gibson*, p. 314.
24. Morpurgo, *Barnes Wallis*, pp. 330–1, 332–3.
25. *New Statesman*, 28 May and 9 July 1955.
26. Harris, *Bomber Offensive*, pp. 163–4, 263.
27. Ibid., p. 261.
28. Brickhill, *The Dam Busters*, p. 194.
29. Ibid., pp. 7, 9.
30. Bennett et al., *The Complete Beyond the Fringe*, pp. 72–4, 116.

2. FILMING *THE DAM BUSTERS*

1. *Picturegoer*, 19 March 1958.
2. Sherriff, *No Leading Lady*, pp. 331, 349, 352.
3. *Picturegoer*, 29 March 1958.
4. Todd, *In Camera*, pp. 100–1.
5. *News Chronicle*, 31 May 1954.
6. Trevor Heelas interview with Michael Anderson, for the BBC series *The Movies*, transcript in British Film Institute Library, pamphlet no. 15784.
7. Gibson to Clark, 2 October 1954; *News Chronicle*, 17 May 1955.
8. Redgrave, *In My Mind's Eye*, p. 238.
9. Redgrave, *Mark or Face*, p. 121.
10. Findlater, *Michael Redgrave, Actor*, p. 136.
11. *Daily Telegraph*, 8 February 1946.
12. Todd, *In Camera*, p. 68.
13. *Picturegoer*, 29 March 1958.
14. *Daily Telegraph*, 21 June 2001.

3. THE FILM: *THE DAM BUSTERS*

1. Harris, *Bomber Offensive*, p. 163.
2. Heelas interview with Anderson.
3. Todd, *In Camera*, p. 70.
4. Fry, *An Airman Far Away*.
5. *Time and Tide*, 28 May 1955; News Chronicle, 2 June 1954.

4. POST-PRODUCTION

1. 'A Life in the Cutting Room', Richard Best interviewed for the BECTU History Project, no. 8, transcript in BFI Library, quoted by permission of BECTU History Project.

2. *Daily Mail*, 2 November 1954; *Kinematograph Weekly*, 17 November 1954.

3. *The Times*, 23 December 1957.

4. Eric Coates, 'The Dam Busters' March' (Chappell sheet music no. 43306, London, 1955).

5. *News of the World*, 22 May 1955.

6. ABPC's press department file on *The Dam Busters*, containing cuttings, press releases, pressbook and campaign manual, is in the BFI Library, ref. 30488.

7. Morpurgo, *Barnes Wallis*, p. 323.

8. *Films and Filming*, March 1955.

9. *Evening Standard*, 19 May 1955; *Evening News*, 17 May 1955; *Star*, 20 May 1955.

10. *Sunday Times*, 22 May 1955.

11. *Observer*, 22 May 1955; *New Statesman*, 25 May 1955.

12. *Daily Telegraph*, 20 May 1955; *Financial Times*, 23 May 1955; *The Times*, 17 May 1955.

13. *Sunday Express*, 22 May 1955; *News of the World*, 22 May 1955; *Daily Mail*, 17 May 1955; *News Chronicle*, 17 May 1955; *Daily Herald*, 20 May 1955; *Daily Mirror*, 20 May 1955.

14. *Daily Worker*, 21 May and 3 June 1955.

15. *Films and Filming*, July 1955; *BFI Monthly Listing*, June 1955.

16. *Today's Cinema*, 15 April 1955.

17. *Kinematograph Weekly*, 21 April 1955.

18. Porter, 'The Robert Clark Account', pp. 469–511.

19. *Sheffield Telegraph*, 13 September 1955, and many other issues, September 1955 to February 1956.

20. *Advertiser* (Adelaide, South Australia), 18–21 May 1943; 12 and 17 November 1956.

21. Todd, *In Camera*, p. 92.

22. *Variety*, 1 June 1955; *Hollywood Reporter*, 22 June 1955.

23. *Motion Picture Herald*, 25 June 1955.

24. *Daily Herald*, 17 November 1955; *Daily Mail*, 18 November 1955; *The Times*, 19 November 1955.

25. More, *More or Less*, p. 181.

26. Jackson, 'Black and White Army'.

27. Morris, *Guy Gibson*, p. 315.

28. Chapman, *The Goalkeeper's History of Britain*, p. 16.

29. Hennessy, 'Modern History in the Making', p. 27.

30. Richard Casey Diary, 28 May 1955, Casey Papers, National Library of Australia MS 6150, series 4, box 28, quoted by permission of the NLA.

Sources

ABPC, Programme for the Australian Première of *The Dam Busters*, held in the library of Monash University, Melbourne.

BBC Television, *War in the Air* (15-episode series, 1954, reissued by DD video).

BBC Television, *The Dambusters* (25-minute documentary, 1993).

British Film Institute Library, Microjacket collection, *The Dam Busters*, ref. 30488 (contains selected reviews, promotional material, and some ABPC press office correspondence relating to the release of the film). The BFI Library has copies of posters, stills and two full scripts for *The Dam Busters*.

DD Video, *Lancaster, the World's Greatest Bomber* (2000).

Royal Air Force Museum, *Dambusters, the True Story* (video, 1993).

ARTICLES AND BOOKS

Bennett, Alan, Peter Cook, Jonathan Miller and Dudley Moore, *The Complete Beyond the Fringe* (London, 1987).

Brickhill, Paul, *The Dam Busters* (London, 1983 [1951]).

Butler, Ivan, *The War Film* (London, 1974).

Chapman, Peter, *The Goalkeeper's History of Britain* (London, 1999).

Coates, Eric, *Suite in Four Movements, an Autobiography* (London, 1953).

Connelly, Mark, *Reaching for the Stars: A New History of Bomber Command in World War II* (London, 2000).

Durgnat, Raymond, *A Mirror for England* (London, 1970).

Eyles, Allen, *ABC, the First Name in Entertainment* (Burgess Hill, 1993).

Findlater, Richard, *Michael Redgrave, Actor* (London, 1956).

Frankland, Noble, *History at War* (London, 1998).

Fry, Eric, *An Airman Far Away* (Kenthurst, NSW, 1993).

Gibson, Guy, *Enemy Coast Ahead* (London, 1988 [1946]).

Harris, Arthur, *Bomber Offensive* (London, 1947).

Hennessy, Peter, 'Modern History in the Making', *Director*, September 1992.

Jackson, Martin, 'Black and White Army: The British at War', *Classic Television*, no. 2, December 1977.

Jones, Richard, 'At Elstree, Realism was the Order of the Day', *ABC Film Review*, August 1954, pp. 28–9.

— 'Elstree Cleared the Runway for *The Dam Busters*', *ABC Film Review*, September 1954, pp. 28–9.

King-Smith, Dick, *The Fox Busters* (London, 1987).

Langley, Oliver, 'The Hazards of Filming *The Dam Busters*', *ABC Film Review*, May 1955, pp. 22–3.

Macfarlane, Brian (ed.), S*ixty Voices: Celebrities Recall the Golden Age of British Cinema* (London, 1992).

More, Kenneth, *More or Less* (London, 1978).

Morpurgo, J. E., *Barnes Wallis: A Biography* (London, 1972).

Morris, Richard, *Guy Gibson* (London, 1994).

Murden, Jeanne, 'Introducing Michael Anderson', *ABC Film Review*, October 1954, pp. 28–9.

— 'Bill Whittaker Talks about *The Dam Busters*', *ABC Film Review*, November 1954, pp. 28–9.

— 'Authenticity and Realism were the Keynotes of *The Dam Busters*', *ABC Film Review*, December 1954, pp. 26–7.

Ottaway, Susan, *Dambuster, the Life of Guy Gibson VC* (London, 1994).

Porter, Vincent, 'Outsiders in England, the Films of the Associated British Picture Corporation, 1949–1958', in Justine Ashby and Andrew Higson (eds), *British Cinema Past and Present* (London, 2000).

— 'The Robert Clark Account: Films Released in Britain by Associated British Pictures, British Lion, MGM and Warner Brothers, 1946–1957', *Historical Journal of Film, Radio and Television*, vol. 20, no. 4, 2000.

Pronay, Nicholas, 'The British Post-Bellum Cinema: A Survey of Films Relating to World War II in Britain between 1945 and 1960', H*istorical Journal of Film, Radio and Television*, vol. 8, no. 1 (1988).

Ramsden, John, 'Refocusing the "People's War": British War Films of the 1950s', *Journal of Contemporary History*, vol. 33, no. 1 (1988).

Rattigan, Neal, 'The Last Gasp of the Middle Class: British War Films of the 1950s', in Wheeler Winston Davis (ed.), *Re-Viewing British Cinema, 1900–1992, Essays and Interviews* (Albany, New York, 1994).

Redgrave, Corin, *Michael Redgrave* (London, 1993).

Redgrave, Michael, *Mark or Face: Reflections in an Actor's Mirror* (London, 1958).

— *In My Mind's Eye* (London, 1983).

Richards, Denis and Hilary St George Saunders, *Royal Air Force 1939–1945: Vol. 2, The Fight Avails*, 3rd edn (London, 1993).

Scott, Lesanne, 'Richard Todd and Michael Redgrave', *ABC Film Review*, January 1955, pp. 30–1.

Sherriff, R. C., *No Leading Lady* (London, 1968).

Sweetman, John, *The Dambusters Raid* (London, 1999 [1982]).

Terraine, John, *The Right of the Line: The Royal Air Force in the European War, 1939–45* (London, 1985).

Todd, Richard, *In Camera: An Autobiography Continued* (London, 1989).